# Some Assembly Required:

## A Networking Guide
## For Women

### Second Edition

Marny Lifshen
and Thom Singer

New Year Publishing, LLC
Danville, California

**Some Assembly Required**

**A Networking Guide for Women**

Second Edition

by: Marny Lifshen and Thom Singer

Published by:
New Year Publishing, LLC
144 Diablo Ranch Ct.
Danville, CA 94506 USA

Copyright © 2016
ISBN: 978-1-61431-048-8

www.newyearpublishing.com

Library of Congress Control Number: 2007930312

*To my husband, Mike. Thank you for believing in me and for being my biggest supporter and my biggest fan. To my daughters, Samantha and Jenna. I am amazed and inspired by you each and every day. Being your mother is my biggest source of pride and joy. Thank you for inspiring me to take chances, help people, and leave my mark on the world.*

*To my parents, Roger and Sylvia Lochhead. I believe that all of my successes, personal and professional, start with my extraordinary parents. You are my heroes, and I am grateful to have you in my life and in the lives of my daughters.*

**Marny Lifshen**

*To all the women who have impacted my life, especially: my mother, Betty Singer; my mothers-in-law, Margo Nistler and Rena Alisa; my wife, Sara Singer; my daughters, Jackie and Kate Singer; my sisters-in-law, Christine Singer, Kris Singer, Yvette Singer, and Margaret Stark; my niece, Summer Stark, my godmother, Mary Shea, my dear friend Andrea Gregg, and so many others who have helped me become the man I am today.*

**Thom Singer**

# Acknowledgements

Working on this book has been a great experience for both of us. While we have been friends for many years, it is a different experience working together on a project of this scope. We have relied on each other's unique strengths to bring this manuscript to life, and hope we have created a book you will enjoy and benefit from reading.

Additionally, this guide could never have happened without Dave and Leslie Morris at New Year Publishing. Their patience, support, and dedication to the project allowed our vision to take shape. As our editor for the original version, Leslie continued to be the taskmaster who enabled our words and ideas to come together properly.

The creation of this book could never have happened without the support of family, friends and colleagues who have been an inspiration to us both throughout our personal and professional lives. Many people directly and indirectly impacted our careers, and taught us about the power of networking. To list everyone would take up an entire book in itself, so we would especially like to thank Thom's father-in-law, Bob Phelan, for his keen eye. Please know that we are grateful to each and every one of you.

# Contents

# Introduction

We have been friends, colleagues, and members of each other's networks for more than 20 years. Our relationship has evolved beyond business into a social friendship, and over time, our spouses and children have become friends. We have turned to each other for advice, referred business opportunities, invited each other to exclusive events, and supported one another in charitable work. We have been co-presenters to a variety of audiences on the topic of networking. But it took serendipity – a chance meeting in the Dallas airport – for us to begin down the path of writing our first book together.

You might wonder why a book about networking just for women is necessary. It's true that the basic philosophy and many of the strategies used in successful networking apply equally to both men and women. It is also true that anyone can learn to become a more effective networker, regardless of gender.

Yet many aspects of networking are not *exactly* the same for men and women. They face different opportunities and challenges in the workplace and in networking. Balancing career and motherhood is just one example. Each gender brings to the table different skills, perspectives and strengths. The way people make, grow, and keep relationships often differs according to gender.

The goal of *Some Assembly Required: A Networking Guide for Women* is to initiate discussions that help women understand and embrace their networking differences. Individual personalities impact networking skills and strategies as much as does gender. We do not intend to create or reinforce stereotypes. Our observations are simply intended to illustrate how networking skills and experiences differ for a majority of men and women. Thom learned first-hand about these differences while speaking to audiences and fielding questions from women. And Marny has experienced these differences while – well, while networking.

We share the same philosophies about developing business relationships and believe that effective, successful networking is:

- For everyone, regardless of career, age, or stage of life.

- A necessary part of everyone's career plan.

- An ongoing process that requires work and commitment.

- Different for everyone.

- A give-and-take relationship.

- A skill that anyone can develop.

We have no doubt that networking can have a significant and meaningful impact on both your professional and personal life. We have experienced its influence ourselves too many times to count, and attribute much of our success to the power of business relationships.

The strategies presented on these pages may appear deceptively simple. Although some of these ideas are basic, few professionals actually do these things on a consistent basis. Career and personal daily responsibilities keep us so busy that it is easy to let our relationships with clients, prospects, colleagues, and others slip into a less important arena. But for those who can successfully cultivate these relationships, there are many rewards to reap.

*Some Assembly Required: A Networking Guide for Women* provides strategies, skills, tips, and resources to help you launch or refine your networking program. It has ideas for all types of women: experienced executives, recent college graduates, entrepreneurs, stay-at-home moms, part-time workers, and women returning to the workforce. Regardless of your individual goals, if you master the networking skills in this book, you will be amazed by the opportunities that will greet you.

You may wonder why a second edition is needed. The simple fact is that networking has evolved in the seven years since we wrote our first book. Social media is just one example – in 2008 LinkedIn was in its infancy and Twitter didn't exist! We have also learned from the countless presentations and workshops we have given over the years, and have added many tools, techniques and ideas to our networking repertoire. We wanted to share these new approaches with you, and a second edition of Some *Assembly Required: A Networking Guide for Women* was the perfect vehicle to do so.

*Marny Lifshen & Thom Singer*
*Austin, Texas*
*September 1, 2015*

**1**

# NETWORKING DEFINED

The term networking is often overused, misused, and misunderstood. There are as many different reasons to network as there are ways to do so; some ways are more effective than others. Each person has different goals for networking: some are professional; some are personal.

Here are samples of common reasons people network:

- Camille's employer has just transferred her to a new city and she is anxious to develop a network of colleagues and friends.

- Jane is thinking of switching careers and wants to build her skills, experience, and contacts in a new field.

- Kayla is ready to purchase her first home and needs referrals on mortgage brokers and real estate agents.

- Allison wants to start her own business and is ready to test the waters with potential investors and customers.

- Jennifer is pregnant with her first child and needs advice on how to balance her career with motherhood, as well as recommendations on everything from babysitters to strollers to pediatricians.

- Caroline has been laid off and needs to identify new job opportunities.

There is no right or wrong reason to network, as long as you understand what networking is, and what it is not. Effective networking is a way of life, not a sporadic strategy that is only followed when you have a specific or urgent need. Think of it like dieting. People diet when they want to lose weight, and while they might succeed, the results are most often temporary. If, however, someone who wants to lose weight makes healthy eating and exercise a *lifestyle*, the results are far more likely to last. By the same token, someone who only networks when they need new clients or are trying to find a new job will not enjoy long-term success.

When you think of networking in the proper context, it is much easier to integrate it into your professional life. We have developed an accurate and relevant definition of networking for you to keep in mind: **"Networking is the process of building and leveraging mutually beneficial relationships."**

Networking IS:

- A verb. It is an active, ongoing pursuit requiring commitment.

- A process. The results are not immediate; it will take time and consistency for you to achieve your networking goals.

- A two-way street. It is a give-and-take relationship, and you must be willing to help people and organizations as much, if not more, than they help you.

- Appropriate and necessary for every type and level of professional at all stages of their career.

- An opportunity to change your career or change your life.

- A lot of work, and also a lot of fun.

Networking is NOT:

- A noun. While it is valuable to have a database of contacts, it is what you *do* with those contacts that counts.

- An occasional activity. It must be a part of your routine to be effective.

- Cold calling or sales. Real relationships cannot be built by phone or social media exclusively, especially if they are one-sided. This does not mean that you cannot sell to people in your network; you just have to know the difference between selling and relationship building.

- Schmoozing or working a room. While you can utilize events for excellent networking opportunities, this is just one small piece of the puzzle.

- A guarantee to improve your professional or personal success. It is a way to set yourself apart and give you many advantages.

- Rocket science. Anyone can improve their ability to build strong relationships through networking.

**"Don't network like a teenager who only talks to his parents when he wants to borrow the car. Networking is about finding people to help first. Eventually, that comes back around. Provide value, stay connected, and then find ways to provide more value."**

**Dr. Mary Kelly**
**Productive Leaders**
**Dallas, TX**

# Networking myths

*Myth 1: Networking is only for times when you are not busy.*

Reality: There seems to be a boom-or-bust mentality around networking. People think that when business is good, they can ignore everyone around them, and that others will naturally understand that they are busy. Conversely, when things slow down, those people rally and try to pick up where they left off. The problem with this philosophy is that if you fail to cultivate a relationship, it will wither away. Jumping in and out of networking comes across as flighty. No one is so busy that they cannot pick up the phone to call people on occasion. So, since you have to eat lunch, schedule it with someone that you want to keep in touch with. If you are too busy to pay attention to your colleagues or friends then you are over-worked, inefficient, or have an inflated view of your own importance.

Many of us can relate to this on a personal level. We've all had girlfriends who are terrific pals and committed friends – until they start dating one person exclusively. Suddenly they are skipping happy hour, not returning calls, and canceling lunch dates. Six months later, when they're single again, they reappear, expecting their friendships to be as strong as ever. Personally or professionally, relationships take ongoing work and commitment – not just when it is convenient.

### Myth 2: Networking is only important if you are in sales.

Reality: Networking can benefit every professional, in every role, in every industry. While sales professionals tend to network naturally, it is critical for everyone. It's a way for you to develop your skills, identify potential employees or partners, connect with peers, and create new opportunities. Networking can also occur within your own company, helping to position you for the future. Look at it this way: your specific job function may not be dependent on networking, but your career probably is. Networking is about building a support system for the long run.

### Myth 3: Only senior executives need a network.

Reality: Everyone can benefit from having a network. As unfair as it may be, women especially need to develop and maintain networks because they do not always have the same advantages that men do in the workplace. For your current job, or for future employment opportunities, you must build your reputation, skills, and relationships *now*. No matter how much experience you have or what your job function is, affiliations with others only have an upside. And remember, while networking, you are not only representing your employer; you are representing yourself. If your employer won't support your networking efforts by giving you the time and resources to join organizations and attend meetings or conferences (shame on them!), find a way to make it happen on your own. You're worth the investment.

*Myth 4: The people you meet networking never refer you business.*

Reality: If you do for others, most of them will return the favor. Many times, however, the benefits of a relationship may not be as clear-cut as someone referring you a customer. It may be that they become an advisor, a partner, a reference, or a friend. They may recommend you for a job or a leadership position within an organization. You may never even know of the favors they have done for you or your career. But if you focus on finding ways to be a valuable resource for them, they likely will do the same for you.

*Myth 5: Networking is unnecessary because if you are really good, success will just come to you.*

Reality: While this may be somewhat true, if you are a "best-kept secret" then you are leaving opportunities on the table. Some people will hear of you because of the quality of your work alone, but if you are not actively advancing your own brand, your reputation, and your network, many other people will not even know you exist. You want to be "top of mind" with many advocates singing your praises!

*Myth 6: You must be an extrovert to be a good networker.*

Reality: While naturally sociable people do have the advantage of possessing confidence and charisma, networking is a set of skills that <u>can</u> be learned and developed. Everyone can succeed at networking if the right strategies and methods are consistently implemented. If large events full of strangers fill you with terror, identify relevant organizations that host smaller meetings. Ask a successful colleague if you can tag along with him or her. Or, focus on building relationships with key influencers one-on-one. If you are new to a job or community, join local clubs that address topics or hobbies that interest you. With time and practice, networking can become a comfortable part of your life, even if black-tie galas aren't your style.

## The four steps of networking

As we have discussed, creating and developing business relationships is a process that takes time and effort. If you think that networking is just "meeting lots of people," the process may seem daunting. But the phases of building successful relationships through networking actually evolve quite naturally, and it's important to not skip or rush through any steps.

## Step 1: Introduce

The first step involves introducing yourself to a new contact
at an event, in a meeting, through a mutual friend, or via
phone or e-mail. While this may seem straightforward
enough, keep in mind that your actions during the
introduction step of networking may well impact your
future relationship.

The introduction is your one and only chance to make a
positive first impression. Here are a few pointers:

- State both your first and second name clearly,
  especially if they are unusual or difficult to pronounce.
  If you do not catch the name of the person you are
  meeting, ask them to repeat it immediately – it will
  save you embarrassment down the line.

- Use eye contact, a friendly smile, and a firm
  handshake. This will ensure you present a confident
  and professional appearance.

- Dress appropriately for the occasion. If you are unsure
  of what to wear, dress a little more nicely than what
  you think is required, as it is always better to overdress
  than to underdress.

- Have a few conversation starters ready to go, in case
  the conversation stalls (see Chapter 6 for suggestions).

- If you are in a meeting, be prepared. For example,
  if you are meeting with a potential vendor that a

colleague has referred to you, research their products or services ahead of time.

- If you are using e-mail or the phone to introduce yourself, plan what you want to say, and be sure to state your purpose for contacting them. Don't fumble around with words or be vague. You can even write this down in advance.

## Step 2: Educate

The education step of networking is your chance to make a connection with a new contact. Your goal should be finding something in common and establishing rapport. It is vitally important that you can talk about yourself effectively. It is not at all unusual for a couple of simple questions to completely stump people as they are chatting with someone at an event – common questions such as "What do you do?" or "What does your company do?" Develop answers to these questions ahead of time and rehearse them so that you are just as comfortable answering them as you are putting on your shoes each morning.

It is also important to remember that the education phase involves two people. Often, people are trying so hard to make a positive first impression that they fail to learn about the other person. You will find that asking creative, compelling questions, as well as talking a little about yourself, will lead you to natural links with others. Be sure to actually listen when they answer; many people simply go through the motions of asking questions and miss the opportunity to learn important information from the answers.

Connections can be on a personal or professional level, so feel free to ask questions outside of business. In fact, some of the most successful professional relationships were started when people discovered that they had a common interest.

---

**Karen was a mid-level HR manager with a large company when she joined the Colorado Women's Chamber of Commerce. During her first meeting, she met Jody, an account executive for an advertising and PR firm. They discovered their shared passion for cooking and Jody invited Karen to attend a meeting of her gourmet dinner club. The two became good friends and often shared personal and professional advice. Four years later, Karen started her own staffing company and hired Jody's firm to develop her marketing materials.**

---

## Step 3: Build

This is where the follow-up happens, and it is here that many networkers stumble. Following up with new contacts takes both commitment and creativity. Sometimes it's clear how to follow up; for example, you are introduced to someone by a colleague and agree to send them information on your products or services. More times than not, however, it is unclear how a relationship will evolve, and you may not know right away if or how you will be able to help one another. Keep these strategies in mind:

- Reach out promptly with an e-mail, phone call, social media or hand-written note after initially meeting someone. They are most likely to remember you if you contact them within a few days of your first meeting. There doesn't have to be a reason for contacting them; getting in touch to say "nice to meet you" is enough.

- Do *something* to keep the connection alive and growing. With time and multiple interactions, you may well discover common ground or an opportunity to work together. If your company has a regular newsletter, ask permission to add them to your distribution list. If you are hosting a relevant event, invite them.

- Look for ways to help them *first*. Building a successful network requires putting others first. Make it a habit to give of yourself before asking others to assist you.

- Be creative as you seek ways to build relationships. Look for organizations, events, or newspaper articles that you think might interest that person, and pass the information along. If something newsworthy happens to that person or their company, send your congratulations; it shows that you are paying attention!

- Be prepared to let go. Not all relationships will develop. Sometimes the interest is not mutual or opportunities to re-connect don't present themselves. It's not personal, so move on and focus on relationships that are evolving.

## Step 4: Maintain

Maintaining relationships with people in your network is often overlooked. Sometimes we take for granted the people that we know the best, and assume that they will be around to support us when we need them. Likewise, we assume they will ask us for help if they need it. In reality, every relationship needs some attention, and you don't want to lose an important ally due to negligence.

**Donna is an attorney practicing banking law. She has a long-time friend and colleague at a local bank who has been her client for many years. There has never been a problem with the quality of her work or her billing rates, so Donna is stunned when her friend tells her that she is going to move her business to a new firm. When she asks why, her client tells her simply that she has become good friends with another lawyer, a fellow golfer. Donna then realizes that aside from work-related meetings and the standard holiday gift basket, she has not reached out to her client in several years.**

Try setting a goal for yourself to proactively connect with key members in your network. It should be every three to four months at a minimum; for the most critical people it should be more often. You do not have to have lunch with each and every one of these people; sometimes just an e-mail or voice-mail message will do. The key is to create a system to follow and to hold yourself accountable.

## Thom Says:

Once you understand and embrace the basics of networking, you are on your way to greater success. Sadly, not *everyone* will embrace networking. This means that you will come across people who will not take the same type of positive actions to forge a mutually beneficial friendship with you. This can be frustrating when you have good intentions and are doing all the right things.

When you encounter someone who is unresponsive to your networking efforts, just be polite and persistent. As you read through this book, we will share some amazing tips and techniques that will allow you to develop and maintain your network, but keep in mind that you cannot force someone to become an active participant.

Continue to reach out to people and become a resource for them, without expecting them to suddenly have an epiphany. If you would like to get to know them better, take a long-term approach. Know that it could take years. Enjoy the process of networking, be sincere and consistent, and enjoy the new people you will meet along the way.

## Marny Says:

One of the most challenging parts of networking for me is maintaining relationships with professional contacts. As a marketing consultant and professional speaker, I must be able to access a diversity of resources for my clients, as well as prospective clients and peer groups for myself. Maintaining those relationships, especially when I don't have an immediate reason to talk to them, has always fallen to the bottom of my To-Do List.

I discovered that the best way for me to keep from neglecting this task was to develop a system. At the beginning of each quarter I identify the 24 most important people that I do not already have regular and frequent contact with. This list includes past clients, referral sources, strategic partners, mentors, and other people in my network. I post this list on my office white board, and each week I reach out to two of the people. I may give them a call, send a quick note, shoot them an e-mail, or meet them for a cup of coffee. The point is that I do *something.* Each week I happily check off two names, and at the end of three months I have maintained 24 relationships. At the beginning of the next quarter, I start all over again.

## FAQ:

**How can I reconnect with someone that I've lost touch with? Should I?**

Absolutely try to reconnect with people. In most cases they will be thrilled to hear from you. The best way to reconnect is to keep it casual. Send an e-mail or phone them to tell them you were thinking of them. Ask questions and listen. Do not wait until you need their help or want to sell them something to reconnect, as they will see right through this.

**How long should I wait before contacting someone a second time if they have not returned my previous message?**

There are a variety of reasons that people will not return your call or email. Be persistent and keep trying to reach them but do not do so at 24-hour intervals. Two or three days is just about the right amount of time. After three unreturned calls, wait two weeks and try again. If you still get no response, you may need to accept that the person is not interested in talking to you.

**How do I effectively prioritize my business relationships to ensure I'm spending the right time on the right people?**

The larger your network, the harder it is to keep up with everyone. Ask yourself if the people you are focusing on can become a mutually beneficial resource. It's not just about who can help you, but also about building relationships with those you can help. Additionally, make sure your friends remain a priority. Never alienate those you really care about in lieu of those who can bring you business.

**How do I figure out how I can help other people in my network?**

Ask. Make it a point to find out what other people are trying to accomplish. If you know what they are trying to do in their professional and personal life, it's easier to connect the dots. You will not always be able to assist them, but not knowing means you can never be a resource.

**What do I do if my boss doesn't support my networking efforts?**

Try educating your boss about the specific organization or events and your goals for becoming involved. Let him or her know whom you expect to meet and what you expect to learn. Show the value your company can gain from your participation. If they still do not get it then you may have to network at early morning events, at happy hours, or at dinner programs.

# 2

# HOW NETWORKING IS DIFFERENT FOR MEN AND WOMEN

Is networking really different for men and women? Absolutely. It's true that the basic philosophy and many of the strategies used in successful networking are suitable for both genders. It is also true that anyone – *yes, anyone* – can learn the skills and become a more effective networker regardless of gender.

The flip side of this, however, is that many aspects of networking are not the same for men as for women. Women can have a different networking experience within the same company or industry, the same organization, or even at the same event as their male counterparts. In many situations, women are excluded – consciously or not – from client lunches, business trips, strategy meetings or casual after-hours gatherings, simply because they're not "one of the guys." Women face different opportunities and challenges in the workplace and in networking. They also bring to the table different skills, strengths and communication styles. The goal of this book is help women understand and take advantage of the inherent differences between the sexes.

## Facing challenges and embracing opportunities

For generations, men have had the advantage of the so-called "Good Ol' Boy Network." Those in this informal, unstructured group of experienced men help each other make connections, gain access to opportunities, and overcome professional hurdles, all of which help them to achieve success. While women have made great strides in the workplace, they still do not have this kind of comprehensive support system. Fortunately, the growth of organizations and events for women continues at a steady pace, and women are attaining more and more leadership roles in business and in their communities. But additional support is needed, especially with regard to the informal mentoring of young women early in their careers.

It would be easy to assume that women are each other's best allies in career development. In many cases this is true; however, you may find it surprising to realize that women also can be our biggest foes, especially those of different generations. The women who broke down the workplace gender barriers during the 1960s and 1970s have a great deal of pride in their accomplishments, and rightfully so. The female innovators of the 1980s also achieved a great deal by winning high-powered leadership roles within corporate America.

Yet each generation does things differently and this has, on occasion, led to tension between the generations. Some women who made great personal sacrifices to build their careers feel that subsequent generations are obligated to do the same, and do not understand when contemporary women choose to pause their career and stay home with their children. Likewise, the trailblazers of decades past who worked 60-hour weeks to attain the first executive roles in Fortune 500 companies can't always relate to women today who work fewer hours—the ones who prefer to take an entrepreneurial path or work for smaller businesses in order to maintain more balance in their lives. These unspoken tensions can make it more difficult for them to work together or to help one another.

Even today, it is not uncommon for a woman to walk into a meeting or event and find herself the only female there. This can be an uncomfortable and intimidating situation, and it can be difficult to gain entrance to a network that is comprised almost entirely of men. But this challenge is actually an opportunity in disguise. Many organizations are looking to diversify and welcome women with open arms. Likewise, committees and boards are often eager to add women to their ranks. Attending male-dominated events can at first be disconcerting, but there is no question that it's an opportunity to stand apart from the crowd. Take advantage of this; confidence and tenacity are key to overcoming gender barriers – real or perceived.

Sharla Frost, a partner in the Houston law firm of Powers & Frost, wrote an article about the challenges female attorneys face when taking a male client to dinner alone. Frost explains that women lawyers are often anxious about this, as in American culture, a man and woman going to dinner together usually indicates dating. She provides great advice on how women can overcome their concerns by simply taking charge of the situation and demonstrating that the dinner is business by:

√  choosing an appropriate (non-romantic) restaurant

√  dressing in business attire

√  meeting the client at the restaurant

√  making arrangements for the correct location of the check in advance of the meal

√  preparing an agenda of topics to discuss during dinner

The need for an article like this demonstrates the fact that there are unique challenges women can face.[1]

# Leveraging your skills and strengths

As we mentioned, some women have different strengths than many of their male counterparts. Instead of blending in with your male peers, capitalize on your dissimilarity. These differences set you apart, and as you may be in the minority in many professional environments, this in and of itself is an advantage.

Let's review some of these strengths, while of course acknowledging that these don't apply equally to all women:

**Attention to detail:** Women tend to notice and remember *everything!* We frequently have the uncanny ability to observe and keep track of multiple details. Used strategically, this can be a huge networking advantage. Paying attention during conversations and retaining the

---

[1]  *National Association of Women Lawyers Journal,* June 2006

information can help build rapport in future interactions.
For example, when talking with someone at an event, it is
advantageous to be able to recall important details such
as when you last met the other person, their profession,
or a recent accomplishment that you read about in the
paper. Consider the power of being able to greet a contact
with "Danielle, I haven't seen you since the UCLA Alumni
Dinner. Congratulations on your promotion to regional
manager!" or "Stella, how did your fundraising project go
with AAUW?" With comments like these, people will know
you are paying attention and will appreciate your effort. It
makes people feel good about themselves, and about you.
Simply put, it shows that they matter.

Women also tend to be better at follow-up, delivering
promised information or promptly scheduling meetings.
We often take the extra time to personalize follow-up
efforts, referring specifically to conversations in a note or
including information that we believe might be interesting
or helpful. Noticing details enables a person to get many
little things right, such as arriving on time for an event,
spelling someone's name correctly, or remembering to ask
an important client about their recent vacation. Make no
mistake; these little things make big impressions.

*The personal touch:* One of the best ways to make a
connection and then build that connection into a successful
relationship is getting to know someone on a personal level.
Things such as asking about family, remembering birthdays,

learning about hobbies and taking food preferences into consideration when choosing restaurants make a positive impression and help develop rapport. In many families, women tend to keep track of personal details like these, as well as following through with buying baby gifts, planning dinner parties, and sending holiday cards. Use this strategy in your professional life as well.

Take the time to learn about the person, and not just their business, and you will likely find common ground. You might have attended the same university, live in the same part of town, or both be yoga devotees. Asking questions will demonstrate your interest in them, and everyone likes to feel interesting! This technique works especially well with men; ask them about their wives, kids, and hobbies, and they'll probably be delighted to talk about these aspects of their lives, as male co-workers don't often ask such questions. You do need to be cautious not to take this strategy too far, however. If you are meeting with a potential customer, for example, it is great to spend a few minutes on personal topics, but be sure to get to the business at hand in a timely fashion, or they might think you are all style and no substance. Balancing the personal chitchat with the brass tacks of business is an acquired skill.

*Multi-tasking:* Networking events and organizations offer a great place for women to utilize one of our most valuable skills – multi-tasking! This skill translates easily into networking. Meeting new people, re-establishing connections with existing contacts, hosting clients or colleagues, and expanding our skills and knowledge through an educational program (all at one event) is certainly achievable. As you set your networking strategy, consider ways in which you can maximize your time and efforts through multi-tasking.

---

**Laura is a partner in an advertising agency and notices that her local chamber of commerce is seeking nominations for women business leaders, who will be recognized at an awards program. Laura immediately nominates her business partner, who is not only a successful business owner and industry leader, but also an active board member of two high-profile community organizations. She then reserves a table at the awards dinner and develops a guest list of referral sources, key clients, potential clients, and freelancers that do work for their firm. At the luncheon, Laura's partner is recognized as a finalist, gaining terrific publicity for their firm and raising her credibility with their guests. Laura and her partner mix and mingle with business and community leaders at the reception prior to the dinner, and then focus their networking during dinner with people who directly impact their business success. This is multi-tasking in action.**

---

*Etiquette expertise:* Whether sending thank-you notes, properly introducing people at events, RSVPing, or returning a call in a timely manner, most women believe etiquette is important. Again, this is an opportunity to set yourself apart and make a positive impression. What are often seen as small etiquette missteps can dramatically affect how you are perceived and reduce your effectiveness in building relationships. Consider how you would feel in these situations:

- Kathy is attending her monthly hospital administrators' association meeting and sees a co-worker, Beth, in conversation with a group across the room. She walks over to join Beth, who makes eye contact and smiles but does not include her in the conversation. After an awkward moment or two, Kathy moves on. *Kathy might brush off the incident, or her feelings might be hurt. Colleagues should always make an effort to help one another, especially at networking events.*

- Denise receives a note from Marcie, whom she met recently at a writers' conference, and quickly notices both her last name and her company's name are spelled incorrectly. *This failure to double-check spelling may cloud Denise's impression of Marcie, even if it seems like a small detail.*

- Sheila is having lunch with two colleagues to discuss potential business opportunities. She can't help but notice that Sue spends most of their conversation texting. This is a case of multi-tasking gone bad! *Sue's behavior is just plain rude, and by not giving her lunch companions her undivided attention, she is telling them that they are less important than the matters at hand on her phone.*

We make impressions each time we interact with someone, and it is important to remember that people are paying attention. Following basic etiquette can make a lasting impression. For more information on networking etiquette, see Chapter 6.

---

**"I have to admit that my personality type makes traditional networking organizations and events hard for me. What I have found that works for me is reaching out to folks with whom I've worked on a one-on-one basis. I love my clients and they seem to return the sentiment. I thank them for their business and ask them to refer Icon as appropriate. We get a huge amount of business from this simple sincere approach."**

**Pamela Myhre**
**Icon Design**
**Boise, ID**

---

## Overcoming our weaknesses

While it would be nice to think that only our strengths as women will impact our networking efforts, the truth is that we do have some weaknesses. Ironically, some of our strengths, if misused in networking, can also be weaknesses:

*Relationship diehards:* Women often take things personally. We tend to put our hearts and souls into our causes. This often leads to meaningful, long-lasting and successful business and personal relationships. Yet sometimes business really is just business. The bottom line has no emotion attached to it. Women should not take it to heart or hold grudges when they don't get the results they hope for from someone they consider a friend or colleague. Taking a business decision too personally can damage an important relationship.

*People pleasers:* Often women, more than men, have a need to please others. This makes us reliable, hard workers who are the first to volunteer when help is needed. While this is a positive trait, it can lead to over-committing and then under-delivering. In turn, this makes us seem unreliable or flakey – the exact opposite of what we want to be known as. To avoid this scenario, carefully assess what you can realistically take on and then make the commitment to exceed those expectations with outstanding results.

*Information sources:* A woman's strength in listening and information recall can be an asset in relationship building. If you establish yourself as a reliable source of information, you will be seen as valuable. However, you need to be careful not to let this deteriorate into gossip. There is a big difference between someone who is well informed and willingly shares relevant information, and someone who spreads rumors, opinions and innuendos. Be careful.

*Loyal friends:* It is not uncommon for women to have close friendships that literally last a lifetime. Our loyalty to and intimacy with our friends creates strong bonds that endure. This closeness can occur with professional friends as well, but it is important to remember that professional networks are only successful if they are inclusive. Women who function in cliques will find limited success with their networking efforts since exclusion is counterproductive. The best networkers excel at making connections with and for others. The more contacts you make and relationships you develop, the more successful you will be.

## When networking crosses the line

Networking is inherently a personal experience; it's all about making connections and building trust. Some of the best friendships come as a result of networking efforts. We all know that people do business with people they know and like, and it's even more fun to do business with friends. But mixing business and pleasure can also be challenging and you should do so only with forethought and caution.

Strong bonds develop from professional contacts all the time so it's important to understand that not everyone in your network can – or should – become a personal friend. Personal friendships require a great deal of intimacy, and this is not always appropriate in a business setting. The nurturing nature of some women makes it difficult for them to draw this line. Additionally, doing business with friends can create awkwardness and distractions when decisions that are in a business's best interest are not in the friendship's best interest. An unsuccessful business deal can result in hurt feelings, compromised trust, and a damaged friendship. Learn to recognize the difference between a personal friend and a professional friend.

**Deanna's biotech company is moving into larger office space and she must find an IT firm to evaluate the company's needs, then build and install a new technology infrastructure. Deanna is thrilled to give an opportunity to her long-time friend, Sylvia, whom she met while volunteering at their local children's hospital. Sylvia's firm wins the bid and the project goes well  at first. Their product recommendations are on point and they stay within budget. But Sylvia's team then misses deadlines for delivery, which were coordinated with the move to the new offices. Problems are compounded by confusion on the subsequent training schedules. Despite Sylvia's best effort to mend fences, Deanna's employer is unsatisfied and the two businesses are at odds over what a fair payment should be. Both sides walk away unhappy. Deanna and Sylvia's friendship is damaged by the conflict, although their personal feelings about one another have not changed.**

Dating can also be an aspect of your life that is directly affected by networking. As a single professional, dating within your network can seem quite natural. After all, the majority of your waking hours are spent in work and work-related tasks. You may very well meet someone who is not in your immediate circle of professional colleagues at an event or through a mutual acquaintance. In this case, dating is unlikely to cause any problems.

However, becoming romantically involved with someone who is an active and ongoing part of your workplace, industry, or network can have serious ramifications. Even if the relationship is solid, you need to consider how people will perceive you. Will they think it is appropriate for you to date a co-worker, customer, vendor, competitor or fellow board member? Will the relationship hurt your career or eliminate other professional opportunities?

It's difficult enough to find a suitable companion without considering how it will impact your professional life; however, if you date someone in your network, you should consider it. If the relationship is unhealthy, or if it ends, the situation can be even more complicated, threatening your ability to remain active in organizations, attend events, work on specific projects, or even remain in your current job. Consider these factors before dating someone in your network. You may still wish to pursue the relationship, but do so with your eyes open.

Women can face additional networking situations that men often do not. Unfortunately, women are still subjected to sexual harassment. While this happens to men as well, it is far less common. While this book is not the forum to discuss such a complex topic, it is important to note that if you ever feel you are being harassed, realize that such behavior is unacceptable. If it occurs, it is important to get advice from trusted colleagues, managers, mentors, or even an attorney.

Women may also be overlooked (both consciously and unconsciously) for jobs and promotions, as well as for leadership positions within organizations and associations. The glass ceiling may not be as impenetrable as it once was, but in some places it is still there. The only right way to address this situation is to proactively and confidently ask for consideration. While no one likes to talk about the awkward, uncomfortable, or unfair situations that can arise between the genders, they are a reality, and women need to be conscious of how they will handle them.

## Thom Says:

When I first wrote *Some Assembly Required: How to Make, Grow and Keep Your Business Relationships,* I did not realize that there were differences in how men and women approach networking. It was from the readers of the book, and from women in the audiences at my speaking engagements, that I became educated about the subtle but important topics that we discuss throughout this book.

I simply was oblivious to these differences. I spent my career building business relationships with both men and women, but I did so from the perspective of a man. I believe that it is common for people to assume that others share their perspective. However, there are many variances that influence how people react in different situations. By accepting and acknowledging the differences, it has opened up my perspective and allowed me to become even more effective at building relationships. The lesson is that no one way is right or wrong, but instead there is power in understanding and respecting each other.

## Marny Says:

My first job out of college was as a marketing and public relations manager for a large, established law firm in Austin. In that role, one of my goals was to get new attorneys involved in community organizations. The local bar association and Austin Chamber of Commerce hosted many relevant programs and events. The Young Men's Business League (YMBL) offered and still offers young professional men weekly educational luncheons with guest speakers and networking through planned social activities. The organization, which was established in the 1920s, also provides members with a way to get involved in the charitable activities, as it supports the Sunshine Camps, a summer camp for low-income youth in the Austin area.

I immediately was drawn to YMBL but was also taken aback that a similar organization did not exist locally for women. I debated the topic with several friends over lunch and we all agreed that while we did not wish to infiltrate YMBL with demands that they allow women members, we needed an organization that provided similar benefits and structure, while addressing our unique issues and interests. The Young Women's Alliance (YWA) was born in 1993. YWA and YMBL operate like peer organizations in many ways, while still recognizing the different needs of their members. I am proud to be a founding member of YWA and served on its board for five years; I encourage other women to create their own infrastructure in their own communities.

# FAQ:

**How do I handle the intimidation of being the only woman at a networking function?**

Recruit a female colleague or friend to attend with you. If that's not possible, gather all your confidence and poise and make the most of the opportunity. Focus on the reasons why you belong at that function that have nothing to do with your gender. Don't try and blend into the background, and don't make a point to try and get noticed either – shoot for somewhere in between.

**How do I know which of my strengths will work well in networking?**

Look at which aspects of your personal life are successful; there is often a correlation between how we handle relationships in our personal and professional lives. The things that you naturally do well in your personal life will translate equally well into your business life. If, for example, you are always bringing new people into your circle of friends, you will succeed at introducing people you know in different business circles as well. If you throw terrific parties, move this skill into planning networking events or serving on the events committee of a charity.

**What do I do if I feel I am being left out of networking opportunities simply because I am a woman?**

First, find out if your assumption is accurate; don't jump to conclusions. Talk to someone that you trust who is familiar with the situation and get their take. Second, ask to be included. In many cases, people are excluded simply because it doesn't occur to others to invite them, and this is especially true for women. Often our male colleagues assume that if we want to participate we'll just ask – as they do! If you still believe you are being discriminated against because of your gender, ask your mentors how to proceed appropriately, and carefully weigh the pros and cons of confronting your colleagues.

# 3

# BUILDING & MANAGING YOUR PERSONAL BRAND

It really is quite amazing how much brands have become a part of society. They are everywhere today, going way beyond cars, fashion and beer. Brands are much more than cool logos, and corporations spend millions upon millions of dollars developing and managing the brands of their products and their companies.

But can you really brand a person? The answer, of course, is yes – and you don't have to be a celebrity to have a personal brand. You have a brand, whether you are aware of it or not. Marketing guru Tom Peters wrote an article for *Fast Company Magazine* in 1997 entitled "The Brand Called You." He was the first to point out that all professionals have personal brands, and he helped us understand how to go about managing them.

So how does all this relate to networking? Every time you attend an event, have coffee with a colleague, or lead a meeting you are putting your brand out there. It is your job to build your brand and to turn it into an asset in your career journey.

## Personal Brands Defined

So how can we explain what a personal brand actually is? First, it's important to understand that strong brands evoke impressions, feelings and opinions. This is true for company and product brands, as well as people. Take, for example, Apple. If we ask you the first words and phrases that jump to mind when you simply see their logo, you are likely to say something like "innovative, trendy, cutting edge, expensive, sleek or cool." These responses are remarkably consistent, even from people who haven't ever owned or used an Apple product. This is because Apple manages every aspect of their brand, from product design to advertising to architecture in their stores. Now let's use this same process for a well-known personality, Ellen DeGeneres. When looking at her photo common responses include "funny, generous, kind, creative or role model." Even people who don't watch her TV show know what her brand is.

> "I've learned people will forget what you said, people will forget what you did, but people will never forget how you made them feel."
>
> – *Maya Angelou*

We believe the clearest definition of a personal brand is how *you* answer the following question:

## "What do I want to be known for?"

It's actually a fairly complex question once you think about it. Of course each of our answers will be different, and there is no right or wrong answer. The key is to really think about what you want your colleagues, customers, clients or friends to say about you. Remember that personal brands are all about impressions, feelings and opinions. In essence, when people talk about you they will say what you are like. Your personal brand is built on the experiences people have working with you.

## Understanding Personal Brands

In order for a personal brand to b effective, they MUST be:

1) Authentic: You have to be you. We'll spend some time talking about how you can adapt and elevate your personal brand, but it is critical to remember that you must be yourself or people will see through it and know something is "off." We all know people who we think are maybe "trying too hard" or simply don't seem sincere – they might be trying to project a personal brand that is not authentic. This definitely affects their credibility even if we can't identify exactly what's wrong.

   So be sure that the personal brand you are putting out there is true to who you are, but be prepared to make small, subtle changes. If you are a naturally quiet, reserved and introspective person, for example, you can't become an outgoing, outspoken and lively person. But, you may need to speak up a bit more, engage with colleagues and take a few more risks in order to elevate your personal brand and achieve your career goals.

2) Distinct: Creating a brand that distinguishes you from others is probably the most challenging aspect of

Jack has just started a new business and he needs a logo, letterhead, business cards and a website. He hires Salina, the owner of a small graphic design business with years of experience in his industry. The project starts off well, and Jack is pleased with the initial designs Salina presents. They agree to a budget and a deadline for completion. Jack soon finds that Salina does not keep him updated on progress and he has to email or call her 3 or 4 times before she responds. She is slow to make the changes that he requests and misses a few. The project takes a month longer than Jack expected, but she does stay in budget. He is happy with the end product, but his experience was frustrating. For Jack, Salina's brand unfortunately does not center around her actual design work, but her customer service. If someone asked him what Salina was like to work with, what is he likely to say?

In thinking about how you answer the question "What do I want to be known for?" think about the following things:

- What makes me different?

- What am I really like?

- What makes me memorable?

- What traits should I emphasize and which should I downplay?

this process. Many of us simply blend in with all the other smart, talented and hardworking professionals. Identifying and communicating what makes you different is difficult, but it is also critical. You can't simply rely on being good at your job and a nice person, because that won't set you apart.

You have to find out what does set you apart—is it your ability to solve problems with creative solutions? Is it your outstanding experience in leading teams through challenges? Is it your skill at making everyone feel valued and motivated to do their best? Or perhaps your talent for taking a complex issue and breaking it down so everyone can understand? As you can see, none of these characteristics focuses on technical skills or job title. Instead, they focus on how you work with others, and the experience others have interacting with you.

> "Start by identifying the qualities or characteristics that make you distinctive from your competition or colleagues. What have you done lately to make yourself stand out? What would your colleagues or customers say is your greatest and clearest strength? Your most noteworthy personal trait?"
>
> – *Tom Peters*

3) Consistent: In order to have a strong, believable personal brand it must be consistent. For example, you cannot present yourself and behave one way with your peers and the people that work for you, but present a different brand to your superiors and customers. Likewise, you cannot separate personal and professional brands. Certainly we all are more casual and relaxed with family and friends then we are in the workplace. But the essence of your brand must be the same, or it will cause confusion and limit your credibility. If you are normally an outgoing, friendly and talkative person you can't then become stand-offish and reserved when you go to the office. You need to be your outgoing self, just turning it down a bit to ensure you are being perceived as professional.

## Elements of a Personal Brand

There are many things you can do to help ensure your brand is being perceived the way you intend, by understanding the key elements that make up your brand. Personal brands are comprised of many elements, both tangible and intangible. These include:

1) Technical skills & experience: While we have emphasized that your personal brand is built on people's experiences with you, your technical talent and experience are definitely a part of the package. Think of your job skills as the foundation upon which

a solid personal brand is built. It is certainly important, but it's not what most people will remember. If you are the best divorce attorney in town but have terrible communication and client interaction skills, this is likely what your clients will remember. If you are a successful sales professional but do not get along with your coworkers, you will probably not be considered for a promotion to sales manager. If you are a manager who has built a reputation as a professional that embraces challenges and juggles many balls successfully, you are more likely to be considered for opening a new location for your company.

2) Demeanor: Simply put, this is what you are like. Your personality, behavior and manner make up your demeanor, and those are a part of your DNA. But there are many small, simple things you can do to adapt your demeanor, if needed. If you are seen as too serious, smile more. If you are seen as uninterested or detached, ask more questions. If colleagues think you are too casual and overly friendly, dress a bit more formally and reduce the personal chatting. These changes may feel somewhat foreign at first, but as long as you are not making drastic changes that are not authentic to the real you, they will help tweak your demeanor in the direction you need. Research shows that "likability" is a growing factor in professional success. By incorporating just a few behaviors that

make you more likable, you can enhance your personal brand while developing allies. Develop and practice your conversation skills; mind your manners; strive to be inclusive and supportive with coworkers; and adapt your approach for particular genders, generations and personalities.

3) Communication style: The way we communicate has a tremendous effect on our personal brand. The good news is that by improving our communication style and skills, we can positively impact our brands and our relationships. We all know that communication is both verbal and non-verbal, but in fact communication is three-dimensional. The verbal component of communication is the actual words you use; the vocal component is the tone you use; and the visual component is the physical cues you give. When broken down, communication is:

- 7% verbal (only!)

- 38% vocal

- 55% visual

As many of us most often use email, texting and social media for communicating with our colleagues, you can see how miscommunication often occurs – we are hoping to relay our message with only 7%! So be aware that the communication tools you choose may impact your brand. For example, many people are very brief in emails and texts, and that could be perceived as curt or rude; it may be more effective to make a call or arrange for a face-to-face meeting. Take a moment to strategize your communication; after all, different people and situations require different tools.

We communicate a great deal with simply our tone or body language. Think, for example, about the word "okay." How many different meanings can that one small word take on just by changing our tone of voice? And we all know how much we can read about a person and their opinions through their body language. Now think about the concept of "confidence." Of course we can communicate confidence with our word choice. But can we also communicate confidence without those words? With our tone of voice, and the way we carry ourselves? These three aspects of communication must be consistent with one another; if our words say confidence, our tone and appearance should as well.

Many aspects of communication can impact your brand. Consider the following questions:

- Does your communication style fit your brand?

- What bad communication habits do you have? (Interrupting? Rambling? Mumbling? Not listening? Emails that are WAAAY too long?)

- How are you most comfortable communicating?

- How can you incorporate strategy into making choices of communication tool choices?

- How can you elevate your communication skills?

4) Physical appearance:

It is easy to say that the way we look doesn't – or shouldn't – matter. But the plain truth is that it does, especially for women. Rather than fighting this, you must accept that your appearance is a part of your personal brand. As we explained, physical cues account for a full 55% of communication, so the way we look certainly impacts the way we are perceived. So make it work in favor of your brand, rather than contradicting it.

Physical appearance isn't about how attractive you are. It is about how you present yourself. While you can absolutely reflect your individual taste and style, every successful physical appearance must be:

Professional: This definition will change depending on each individual's profession, industry, company and city. Professional means something very different to a software programmer in San Diego than to a corporate recruiter in Chicago. The important thing is to make sure you look like a professional within your own circumstances, and that you are ready for most business occasions. Women have a lot more options than our male colleagues when it comes to dressing for work, but we need to be sure not to take this too far. The phrase "dress for success" may be a bit cliché, but it still applies!

Modern: You must look like you are a part of today's workforce, and your wardrobe and style should reflect that. While some pieces are classics that still apply today, make sure your clothing, hairstyle and accessories don't say "I began my career in 1998 and I haven't been shopping since!"

Well groomed: Being tidy and put together is a sign of respect for yourself and for the people you work with. It makes it look as though you took time and care with your appearance, which makes you look like you have it together. This applies to not only your clothes (which should be clean, unwrinkled and fit you well), but to your hair, make-up and accessories such as shoes and purse.

5) Your network:

Of course your network is a part of your personal brand! After all, you are judged (in part) by the company you keep. Does your network reflect your brand? Many of us tend to build our network with peers, but you also need to build your network UP. Make sure your network includes colleagues that have brands similar to yours, as well as those that have the kind of brand you'd like to have in the future. If you want to be perceived as an industry leader, spend time in the company of other leaders.

# Five steps for creating an effective personal brand

Understanding, evaluating and elevating your personal brand may seem daunting, but it is entirely doable by following five straightforward steps. Any changes you do want to make will likely be quite small. The hardest part is making the commitment.

1) Define your current brand: how would you define your brand today?

   Briefly summarize what you believe your brand to be; your top strengths; your key characteristics; what you think your reputation is with colleagues. You can simply write words and phrases, or complete sentences.

2) Determine how others perceive you: what do *they* say your brand is?

   Identify 3 or 4 trusted people to ask what they think your brand is. Do not include good friends, your supervisor, or people who report to you, as that might create an awkward situation. Do ask mentors, former co-workers or clients, or people you serve on boards or committees with. Ask them what they would say if someone asked them about you. Ask them what your key strengths and weaknesses are. This can be scary, but remember you will learn more positives than negatives! It's crucial to understand how your brand is being perceived, as it may not be as you intend. And, if you don't have a clue what your brand is or should be, this will help you to begin crafting one.

3) Identify your brand heroes: what do you value/admire?

Name 3 or 4 people that you especially admire, and then figure out what it is about them that you are drawn to. Is it their positive attitude, or the fact that they are always growing their knowledge and skill sets? Is it their work ethic or their ability to command a room? These brand traits are clearly something you value, and you may be able to integrate these into your own brand. They may also be skill sets you must first develop, and can then incorporate into your brand.

4) Clarify where you want to go: how do you answer the question "What do you want to be known for?"

Based on the insight you have learned from the previous three steps, you now get to determine how you want to evolve your personal brand. The best place to start is by answering that key question, and integrating some of the new information into it. This is what you want people to be saying when asked about you a year from now. Again, there is no formula – just write down what you want to be know for!

5) Create a plan to close the gap: how are you going to get there?

Now for the final, crucial step; you need to identify ways you can proactively and consistently close the gap between where your brand is now and where you want it to be. It is important that you include only specific, achievable action steps, instead of big picture, visionary items. It may appear at first that the gap is large, but it's usually overcome with focused, subtle behavior changes. For example, you may think you are presenting yourself as a strong, knowledgeable leader, but you may actually be perceived as a domineering know-it-all who is not team-oriented. The gap may seem huge, but by simply asking your team for input more often, regularly acknowledging their contributions, and including them more in decisions you can effectively change your brand.

## Thom Says:

Whether you have paid attention to your personal brand or not, you have one. People in the business community are always watching, judging and making assumptions. What you say, what you do, and how you make people feel are always important. Have a bad day and treat someone poorly and that person, and anyone else who witnessed your behavior, will brand you with a negative label. I have seen many well-intentioned people develop a poor reputation because of one or two bad choices in how they interacted with another person.

While we are always growing and changing as people, others only have a few glimpses into our lives to form their opinions. As we expand our abilities, skill sets, and improve ourselves, the world will not necessarily witness our metamorphosis. Thus you have to be keenly aware of your personal brand at all times, as it can be hard to change it down the line.

## Marny Says:

When I made the career change from marketing communications consultant to professional speaker, I knew I'd have to evolve my personal brand. As I followed the steps outlined above, I was a little taken aback at how many small changes I needed to make. I learned some things about the way that I was perceived that surprised, gratified and humbled me. I learned what characteristics to play up, and which to play down. I got great advice on how to grow my energy, elevate my appearance and leverage my natural strengths. I think that one of the keys to my success is that I have always been true to my authentic brand. Whether I am speaking to a conference of 1,000 attendees, leading a workshop for 25, or meeting with a client one-on-one, I am still just me. I might tweak the specifics, but because I am authentic I am comfortable, and because I am comfortable so is everyone else.

# FAQ:

**How do I know what communication skills I need to improve?**

Ask the people you work with – they'll tell you what your bad habits are! Once you know, you'll start to recognize when you do them, and that's the first step in changing them. Don't be afraid to ask for professional help in developing more complex communication skills such as negotiations or presentations – it's an investment that will pay off.

**Once I have the brand that I want, how do I manage it moving forward?**

Think of your brand as a benchmark – something you measure professional activities against. If you are asked to join the board of an organization, for example, ask if that helps or hurts the brand you have built. Does it fit? Just being aware of and invested in your brand will help you evaluate and adapt it in the future.

**What do I do if I need to update my appearance but can't afford an image consultant?**

Ask the people whose style you admire where they shop, where they get their hair cut, etc. You're not trying to become a replica of these people, but you can certainly get some pointers from them. Also, take advantage of the professionals who work in shops and department stores – they are the experts, so let them suggest how to find the right look for you, from clothing to accessories to make-up.

**What if the gap between how I want to be known and how I am actually perceived is HUGE?**

It probably won't be, so don't fret! But even if it does seem like a big gap, small and steady changes in your behavior, communication, appearance and demeanor can make a real change. It doesn't have to be dramatic – in fact it's better if it's not – but by committing to little tweaks, you'll get to the brand you are after.

"Essentially your brand is the way you wish people to feel about you. I believe you start by identifying your core values, then use them to create a mission for your professional life. Make sure that all your behavior and communications are consistent with those values, and keep your brand alive by finding ways to put it out in the world through personal connections, social media and community involvement."

**Pam Sherman**
**The Suburban Outlaw/Sherman EDGE**
**Rochester, NY**

**4**

# GETTING STARTED IN NETWORKING

As you start your networking journey, you will come across many opportunities to interact with exciting and interesting people. To give yourself the best chance of long-term networking success, there are some steps that you can take.

First, figure out where you are now. Being honest is important, as it allows you to accept your strengths and weaknesses. By knowing yourself, you can be more valuable to those around you. Second, identify where you want to go. A boat on the ocean can go many places, but without a planned destination, it can be forever lost at sea. Third, draw your map. Think in advance about what it will take for you to establish strong relationships with other people in the business community. Be realistic about the time and effort that it will take. Fourth and finally, check every now and then to make sure you are still headed in the right direction. It is easy to get caught up in the process and lose sight of why you are networking in the first place. In other words, assess your status, define your goals, make a plan, and evaluate your progress.

## Four Keys to Networking Success

In speaking to and working with a wide variety of professionals across the country, we soon saw that many were facing common obstacles. The comments we consistently hear go something like this:

"I just don't understand how networking will help me – I don't know why I'd do it."

"I don't know where to start! Where do I go to network?"

"I just don't have the time."

"I don't know how to network – I don't think I am the kind of person that can be good at it."

These common themes lead us to identify four keys to networking success.

1. Motivation

2. Direction

3. Time

4. Confidence

## Setting your networking goals

Each of us has different reasons for networking, as well as our own way of determining what success looks like. The good news is there are no right or wrong reasons for networking. This book will help you play to your strengths to grow your network. As we walk you through some goal setting, remember that not everything we talk about will be appropriate for your situation. But do not skip this step, since determining where you are going is an important element in achieving your goals. Without a clear goal, you may not recognize success when you see it.

To define your networking goals, you must figure out what you want as an end result. Why do you want to be a better networker? You will probably have multiple reasons, perhaps a blend of personal and professional ones. Think beyond "to help my career" or "to expand my circle of friends." Drill down by asking yourself questions that clarify your goals. Do you want a larger and more influential peer group? Why? How will they help you? How can you help them? Do you want to gain new business for your company? What kind? Who are the decision makers? Where can you meet them? Write your answers down and revisit them often. As your career and life evolve, your answers to this question will as well.

Be sure to include organizations, events and individuals in your networking goals, and be as specific as possible. Identify the groups you want to get involved with, the events you want to attend and the people you want to meet. You don't need to know the names of people to set your networking goals; you can just identify the type of professionals you want to meet, such as marketing executives, small business owners, or women in the engineering profession.

"I enjoy going to conferences to develop strengths in new areas and stay current on trends in my field, but they can be daunting. Before I go to an event, I set a personal goal for myself, such as 'make at least 2 new connections.' It helps to keep me focused on networking and gives me a little nudge to put myself out there."

**Marissa Steinberger**
**Jack Kent Cooke Foundation**
**Landsdowne, VA**

## Make the commitment and make the time

It can be a challenge to integrate networking activities into a full dance card, especially if you are a working mother already struggling to balance your career and family. The secret here is to first make networking a priority, then create a plan, and finally, make it a habit.

Adjust your mindset to include networking as a required part of your job, short-term and long-term. Put it on your to-do list and on your schedule! Now relax. Networking does not have to take an inordinate amount of time.

The key is to be realistic about your resources – time, money & energy. Most of us have limitations on all three, so you need to keep these limitations in mind when developing your networking plan and determining your priorities.

If you are just starting out in networking or if your circumstances have changed, here is a basic plan that will work within even the tightest schedule:

1. Choose the one organization that is most relevant to your career or industry and be an *active* member. Most organizations only have one meeting per month, so commit to attend regularly. If you have young children, line up a regular sitter for those dates so it'll be harder for you not to attend. If you can add a second organization which will expose you to a broader group of professionals, that will be even better.

2. Hold meetings – coffee or lunch are fine – at least twice a month with important contacts. Review your contacts regularly to make sure you're not overlooking people you haven't seen in a while. You don't have to have a specific agenda beyond building or maintaining your relationship.

3. Identify the two or three key annual events in your community or industry, and commit to attend each year. It doesn't matter whether it's a black-tie dinner or a two-day software conference; figure out which events are critical and put them on your schedule.

4. Combine multiple meetings into one. If there are three or four people with whom you have been meaning to meet, ask yourself if you could schedule one luncheon with them all. If they don't already know each other, perhaps they should!

5. Contact two people in your network each week by e-mail, phone, social media or hand-written notes. You don't have to be face-to-face to keep relationships intact.

It is better to fully commit to a limited number of networking opportunities than to sporadically participate in many. Set goals that are realistic and hold yourself accountable. Try to involve your friends or colleagues in your networking; if you arrange to meet up with someone at an event, or join an organization with a colleague, you will be more likely to follow through.

Some people find it helpful to actually schedule networking time on the calendar – thirty minutes or an hour of dedicated time each week when they catch up on social media, return emails, schedule networking meetings, check on organizations and events, and do reach-outs to their network.

While making a commitment to networking may seem daunting, it really is quite manageable once it becomes a habit. The key is to reach out to people you don't already see or talk to on a regular basis; grabbing coffee with a co-worker or calling a client is important, but it doesn't constitute networking.

# Tracking, evaluating and revising your networking plan

It is equally important to regularly step back and evaluate your networking plan every six months to make sure it's delivering the results you're after. Make a habit of doing this the same weekend you move your clocks forward and back.

The benefits of networking may seem intangible at times, which is why tracking your results will help keep you motivated. Consider keeping a "Networking Diary." When you attend an event and meet new people, jot their names in the diary, along with notes about potential opportunities and how you might follow up with them. If you learn about a promising group to join or think of an idea for an article or speech, record these as well. It will help prompt you to actually follow up while tracking which events and organizations are giving you the best contacts.

Neither Rome nor a network was built in a day. One of the most common mistakes that people make in networking is having unrealistic expectations about when they will see results. Relationships are developed over time as rapport and trust are built. The people we meet do not run back to their office and search their databases for leads to send to us. Opportunities to help people sometimes do not present themselves for months or even years. Be patient, be consistent, and stay focused on the big picture.

While you do not want to keep an official scorecard, you do want to evaluate how the people in your network are helping you. Each of us only has a certain amount of time to invest in building relationships and, while we want to be polite to everyone, there are people who never give anything in return. Learn to identify these people. If you find yourself sending a lot of business to someone or assisting them regularly and they tend to be too busy to reciprocate, focus your energy elsewhere.

You should also evaluate the organizations and events with which you are involved. Don't simply renew your membership or sign up to attend an event out of habit. Are you meeting the kind of people you want to through these functions? Are you getting the education, skills, and leadership opportunities you need? If not, you may need to attend different events, join different groups, or simply figure out a way to get more out of your current involvement.

### Thom Says:

The choices of where to network can be overwhelming. In most large cities there are dozens, if not hundreds, of groups that you could get involved with to make connections. I have discovered that you cannot accurately judge a group until you are actively involved; this sometimes leads to disappointment when you realize the organization is stagnant or not living up to its mission.

I was involved with an organization that had a great national presence. Sadly, the local chapter was not doing very well. There were many members, but few participated in the meetings. Additionally, the programs did not educate or inspire those who were in attendance.

Because I believed there was potential in this organization, I used the opportunity to work with a friend to revitalize the chapter. We actively recruited other key people to get involved and scheduled top-tier speakers to address important topics. The mission of the group was positive, and the influx of new members helped reenergize the meetings.

Attendance grew and long-time members came out to participate again.

Instead of just running from a group that does not meet your needs, consider helping to improve the organization.

## Marny Says:

At a networking event a few years out of college, my then-mentor pointed out a woman in the crowd to me. "That," she said, "is Carol Thompson. She is president of the board of directors of the chamber of commerce, and is one of the most influential business leaders in Austin. You need to get to know her." After my mentor introduced us, I followed up and then sought Carol out at other events. I also offered my services as a volunteer for the Chamber. Eventually, the law firm for which I was working hired Carol as a marketing consultant. We worked closely together and following that, she hired me. Six years later I became a partner in her firm, The

Thompson Group. Carol has been an invaluable advisor, colleague, friend, and inspiration to me over the years.

I share this story to encourage you to reach for the stars when identifying the individuals you'd like to meet and mimic in your professional life. Don't be afraid to approach people simply because their status is above yours; remember that you bring something to the table, too. If someone had told me when I first met Carol that I would one day be her business partner, I'd have thought the idea impossible. But, I was also young and fearless enough not to be intimidated by her position. Most people do want to help others, even if it is just by passing on some advice during a conversation at an industry meeting. The only way you're certain not to learn from those you admire is by not asking.

# FAQ:

I often find myself putting networking on hold while I deal with the crisis *du jour*. And as a working mother, that's more often than not! How do I change this habit?

There are two easy ways to make networking a regular priority. First, simply consider networking an appointment you are committed to, whether attending an event or meeting a colleague for lunch. Stop thinking of it as an optional item on your calendar. Second, join an organization or arrange to attend an event with a friend or colleague. If you have made the commitment to meet someone, you are far less likely to blow them off than if you are only answering to yourself.

**If I believe I'm doing all the giving in a particular business relationship, how do I ask this person to help me in turn?**

Have you actually asked for help? Most people are happy to help if you just ask. It may not even occur to them unless you spell it out. Additionally, you may want to gently remind them about how you have helped them, and then be as specific as possible with how they can help you. If they can't or don't follow up, it's probably time to focus your energy on others.

**How do I get directed to the right organizations and events for me?**

First and foremost, ask your coworkers, your friends, your boss, your mentors. If you reach out to people who are in the same industry or profession, they will certainly tell you about organizations they are involved with and events they attend. But be ready to talk about your networking goals when asking for direction!

# 5

# TOOLS OF THE NETWORKING TRADE

Now that you have defined your networking goals and developed your strategy, it's time to put your plan into action. Are you ready to dig in? There are several effective tools that will ease you into active networking, and help you be more confident and effective.

## Tools for networking events

**Business Cards:** Your business card is your single most important tool. Despite all of the technology advancements and apps on your smart phone, business cards are still the best way to share contact information between professionals. Carry your card with you at all times. You never know when you'll meet someone new or run into an old acquaintance, and your card is an easy and unobtrusive way to be sure they take away something useful from your conversation. Networking opportunities happen in all sorts of environments, from business functions to the dentist's office or the grocery store, and from dinner parties to your child's soccer games.

In addition to containing your pertinent contact information, your business card is an opportunity to make a positive impression. It helps someone develop an interest in your company or services, and sets you apart. While it is increasingly common for professionals to simply transfer contact information from business cards to PDAs or databases, your card still gives you the chance to introduce or reinforce your personal brand.

Here are some business card pointers:

**Make sure your business card looks professional.**
Business cards are a part of your image. If you don't
have a lot of experience in marketing or graphic design,
hire a designer to create your card. There are many
talented and affordable freelance graphic designers, and
this is an investment that will pay off. Online services
such as Vistaprint.com are another affordable option.

**Make sure your contact information is up to date.**
You do not want to be scratching off old data or
hand writing in a new phone number; it brands you
as disorganized and unprofessional. Don't forget
to include your e-mail address and website, and
appropriate social media links.

**Use color on your card.** Years ago, having color on
your business card was cost-prohibitive. Today color
is inexpensive and will help to make you and your
business card memorable. Many professionals still
subscribe to the idea of having raised black ink on a
white or beige card. If this is you, know that you will
not stand out. Finally, leave the reverse side of the card
a light color or white so people can jot notes on it if
they wish.

**Be brief.** Your business card is not your resumé or
a marketing brochure. If too much information is
included, people will be less likely to read it. If the card

is cluttered, or contains gimmicky slogans or photos, it will appear unprofessional. If you do a good job of introducing yourself and making a connection, your name, company and basic contact information on your card should be enough to trigger a reminder.

**Use the standard size and shape.** If your card has an unusual shape or size, it is difficult to file, and thus might not make it back to the recipient's office or contact database.

On the practical side, let's talk about where you should carry business cards when attending an event. Many skirts, dresses and suits (let alone evening gowns) do not have pockets. This is when you pull out your secret weapon, a small handbag to use in lieu of your everyday purse. In this bag carry *only* your business cards, your keys, your phone and a lipstick. This will solve your pocket problem, and will eliminate that awkward delay of searching for your cards in your regular purse, which probably contains many other items. It's also a good idea to buy a few suits with pockets. While men typically have seven pockets in their suits, women have to be more creative in making sure that they have a spot to put their cards.

**Name tags:** The purpose of wearing a name tag at an event is to facilitate conversations. Knowing someone's name and whom they work for makes it easy to start a conversation. You easily can approach someone with "Hi, Bill, I have a friend that works for Exxon," or "Mary, I haven't heard of The Hill Group. What does your company do?" Many times, people choose not to wear name tags (or, frighteningly, the organization hosting the event does not provide them) or the text is too small for the average person to read. This is a missed opportunity since people are more likely to approach someone new when his or her name is in plain view.

Keep these tips in mind for the next time you write your own name tag at an event:

1. **Make it legible.** Print clearly and neatly.

2. **Make it informative.** Include your first and last name, with your company's name underneath. Be sure to use the version of your company's name that most people will recognize, avoiding internal nicknames or initials if they are not widely known. If you work for Hewlett-Packard, people will know what HP is, but abbreviating Whole Foods to "WF" means nothing to the masses.

3. **Make it visible.** Wear your name tag where it can be easily seen – not on your belt or down near your hip. If you are wearing a jacket or coat, do not place it on your shirt. Instead, put it on your outermost piece of clothing. The best place is on your right shoulder, as when you are shaking hands with someone it is a natural line of sight along the outstretched arm to the shoulder.

**A Personal Tag Line:** As we discussed in Chapter 2, it is not uncommon to stumble when answering simple questions like "What do you do?" or "What does your company do?" While you certainly *know* the answer, verbalizing it in a clear, compelling and concise manner is a bigger challenge. And here is a tip: the answer is NOT to recite the title on your business card!

There are two keys to conquering this challenge effectively:

> *The first is to think about the question in a new light, and compose answers that are relevant yet different.* Avoid industry jargon or long, overly technical explanations; your goal is to find an original description of what you actually do, who you do it for, and why.
>
> Consider these very different answers to the standard question "So, what do you do?"
>
> *Good:* I work for a bank.
>
> *Better:* I'm a mortgage broker.
>
> Best: I assist people in making what is usually the single biggest purchase of their lives — their home.
>
> *Good:* I work in high tech.
>
> *Better:* I'm in HR for a multi-media software company.

*Best:* I'm in charge of employee retention for a great company called Tech for Girls, where we develop educationally oriented interactive games for pre-teen girls.

*Good:* I work for an ad agency.

*Better:* I'm a media buyer for Moeller and Stevens, an ad agency.

*Best:* I'm a media buyer for Moeller and Stevens, an advertising agency specializing in creating and launching affordable advertising campaigns for small retail businesses.

*The second key to success with a personal tag line is to rehearse it until it flows naturally.* As you wrestle with a unique way to talk about your job and your company, try writing different versions down on paper. This will help you refine your ideas. Practice your tag line with your spouse, friends or co-workers and get their feedback. There can be a fine line between interesting and cheesy, and you'll need someone you trust to tell you if you've crossed it. Once you have refined your tag line, practice, practice, practice. Taking the time to perfect your presentation will make you more comfortable and confident when it comes time to say it to someone you don't actually know.

Remember, your personal tag line is always a work in progress so update and amend it as necessary. Your goal is to deliver relevant information while capturing the interest of a new contact.

**Media:** If you are to be a successful networker, you must be able to participate actively and intelligently in conversations. Whether you are mingling at an event or sitting at a conference table, you should be able to converse about current events. To do this, you must read the news on a daily basis, whether online or on paper.

Imagine this scenario: While attending a conference, you take a seat at the luncheon table to find that all your peers are talking about the acquisition of a major player in your industry. Since you know nothing about the company or the acquisition, you are unable to participate in the discussion. This scenario is played out in networking events each day. When you are not up to date about what is happening in the world, you are at a disadvantage.

With so much information available online, there is no excuse for not keeping up with important news. Read the local news each day, scanning each section and reading the business section completely. If your community has a weekly business journal, add that to your required reading list. Also, it is also wise to read respected national news publications such as *Time, US News & World Report* and *Newsweek*. And finally, read the publications that are specific to your industry or profession. A balance of media is best, and will help insure that you can connect through conversation while networking.

Additionally, it can also be a distinct advantage for women to keep up with the major sports stories. Men often outnumber women at networking functions, and sports are a common topic of discussion. You don't have to be an expert, or even really like sports (although it certainly helps if you do); you just need to know what people are talking about. If you are knowledgeable about sports, you can engage actively in conversation with male colleagues and stand out.

Finding the time to be well read is a challenge. Like anything, if you make reading a regular part of your schedule, it will become easier. If you fall behind on reading periodicals, throw away back copies and start fresh with the most current issues. Devoting 30 minutes each day to your reading should be enough to stay current.

## Follow-up Tools

**Letters and e-mails:** One of the best ways to follow up with someone is to send them a short handwritten note. In today's digital world, a handwritten note has become rare, and thus more memorable. Here is an example:

> *Dear Colleen,*
>
> *It was a pleasure to talk with you at the Pacific Manufacturers Association dinner. I enjoyed learning about your company and wish you much continued success. Please let me know if I can ever be of any assistance. I hope to see you at another PMA function in the near future.*
>
> *Best wishes,*
> *Judy Jones*
> *Simon Electrical, Inc.*

Consider sending correspondence that will really set you apart. If, for example, you read an article that features or even just mentions a person whom you know well, clip this article and send it to that person with a note. He or she will be flattered that you took the time to pass it on. This strategy also works if you read an article that a member of your network would find interesting. For example, if you read a story about a traveling art exhibit coming to your city in a few months, and know someone who loves the artist, clip and send them the article. If the piece is online, e-mail them the link with a note saying, "Thought you would enjoy this article." Be sure not to forward mass e-mail links to your entire database, though; that does not show any personal thought and is instead, annoying.

"When we started vcfo, the first business purchase I made was for vcfo-branded note cards. I remember telling someone that I felt we would get more business from those cards than from almost any other effort. I consistently use them to thank people who help us, to congratulate those who are having a success, and to stay in touch with individuals who are important to the company. I have not let email replace sending a hand written note from time to time, and I credit that with some of our success."

**Ellen Wood**

**CEO, vcfo**

**Austin, Texas**

Following up with an e-mail is the quickest way to reach out after meeting someone, but you do run the risk of your message getting lost in Spam or in the dozens of e-mails that person receives each day. While some people read e-mail immediately, many others have hundreds of messages hanging out in their inbox, so it could be weeks before they read yours. And, if you're among the majority that do not spell check your e-mail, you could hurt your professional image. Keep your e-mail brief, reminding the person about where and when you met, and suggesting or confirming next steps. Do not include several screens of information or attach a brochure. A follow-up e-mail is not a solicitation for business, but rather a vehicle for you to convey how much you enjoyed your initial meeting.

**Brochures and Newsletters:** When someone you have met indicates that they are interested in learning more about your company, sending them a follow-up letter and enclosing a brochure is a great next step. Brochures can provide the information on your company's products or services, including lengthy details that aren't appropriate for a follow-up letter or e-mail. A well-made brochure can be an outstanding device for the educational phase of networking, but remember that it only plays a supporting role until you make it relevant for its recipient: it's too general to be truly valuable.

Newsletters, either electronic or printed, can be another great way to demonstrate your expertise to clients, prospects, referral sources and business partners. However, so many companies now have some form of newsletter that you need to find a compelling reason for people to read yours. It should include timely, helpful information in a well-designed format, and it also requires some kind of hook. By law, you must give people the option of being removed from your electronic distribution list. There are services such as Constant Contact that can manage this for you. (See Chapter 9.)

**Celeste, a psychologist in private practice, has created a monthly newsletter for customers and friends. In addition to its standard content, it also includes a trivia quiz of little-known facts about her city and its neighborhoods. Readers can e-mail or call in their answer, and on the 15th of each month she has a drawing to award a $100 gift certificate to a local restaurant. She regularly receives dozens of correct responses! In the newsletter the following month Celeste reveals the answer and the name of the winner. This is a memorable hook.**

**Websites & Blogs:** Let's be honest for a moment. When we meet someone new or run into a former colleague, we go back to the office, fire up our browser and look at his or her company's website. Websites are a good source of information on a company and its people. Well-designed, professionally-written websites can provide a reader with a solid overview of a company's mission, and can play a part in a person deciding whether they want to pursue a relationship further.

Many individuals are also now designing their own personal websites & blogs. A blog is an online journal. Savvy networkers use their blogs to demonstrate their knowledge and experience, and to promote their personal brands and establish themselves as thought leaders in their area of expertise. You can also look for opportunities to provide guest blogs to relevant organizations and associations that are looking for valuable content to share with their members.

Blogging involves a time commitment to regularly create relevant posts that provide value and encourage readers to keep coming back. If you are successful, your blog becomes part of your networking efforts and your personal brand.

If you are going to maintain a website or blog, the content must be professional in nature. Keep in mind, people and businesses consistently use online searches to research those with whom they do business or hire. There's a business-appropriate way to utilize blogs and social media, as we will discuss in greater detail in Chapter 9.

**Résumés and Bios:** While most companies have brochures and websites to describe their business offering and target market, they rarely provide much information on individuals who work for the company, unless it is the management team or board of directors. Résumés and bios are tools that focus on *you*.

Résumés are a short review of your education and career, including dates and job specifics. While résumés are most commonly used for job hunting, they also are needed for pursuing internal promotions, and can also be a useful tool when you are being considered for a board position with a charity, a for-profit company, or an industry association.

Bios are more of a general summary of your experience and expertise, and are usually in paragraph form. Rather than listing the names of your employers and dates of your employment, bios emphasize the highlights of your career and your special skills. They can be especially useful if you are trying to secure speaking engagements or by-lined articles in print or online media. Both your résumé and your bio should include your membership and leadership roles in professional and community organizations.

**Your Networking Tool Kit should include:**

- Accurate, memorable and professional business cards

- A clear, original and well-rehearsed personal tag line

- Knowledge about current events and industry news

- Well-written follow-up letters and e-mails

- Appropriate, updated and strategic websites & blogs

- An updated and focused résumé and bio

## Thom Says:

When I released my first book, *Some Assembly Required,* I decided to start a blog to help with search engine optimization. What I did not realize was that the blog would become a major credibility tool in launching my professional speaking career and a powerful aid with my general networking efforts. Posting three to five days a week has dramatically improved my writing skills. Additionally, I have now created hundreds of short essays that can be adapted for magazine articles or future books.

In my blog I regularly share my thoughts and observations on a variety of business and social topics. Over time, readers get a clear picture of who I am and I've been told that they feel a strong connection to me.

The blog is also a chance for me to follow up with people I meet when networking. If the topic of my blog comes up in a conversation, sending that person a note or e-mail with the URL is an easy next step.

*The Some Assembly Required Blog* (www.thomsinger. blogspot.com) has become an important part of my personal brand. I hope you will log on and read it soon!

## Marny Says:

While in my senior year of college, I volunteered for the events committee for the inauguration of the late Texas governor Ann Richards. As we were setting up for one of the inaugural balls, the soon-to-be governor honored us with a quick visit, where she personally thanked each of us for volunteering. I stood in line, excited to meet such an outstanding leader and engaging personality. When she reached me, Governor Richards fixed her piercing blue eyes on me, smiled warmly, gave my hand a firm shake and then promptly ripped my name tag off my left shoulder and slapped it on my right. She made me shake her hand four times, until it was strong and energetic enough, and then demonstrated how the eye easily travels to the right shoulder to read a name tag. Needless to say, I have never forgotten this particular networking lesson!

# FAQ

What is the most appropriate time to give someone my business card and to ask for theirs?

There is not a single most appropriate time to exchange business cards when meeting someone new, but it is often most comfortable when you are first introduced. This is especially helpful if your name or company name is unusual, as the person you are talking to can refer to it. You can also exchange cards when you are parting ways, saying, "It was great to meet you. Here's my card; do you have one?"

**Is it a good idea to have a permanent plastic name tag produced for me to wear to all networking events?**

While a permanent name tag would certainly set you apart at events, it could be viewed as a bit tacky, and reminiscent of employees at retail stores. We recommend using the name tags provided at events.

**How can I create a personal tag line if I don't have a job?**

Many people network while looking for a job, so don't let this dissuade you. Include your profession or industry experience in your tag line, and state simply and confidently that you are currently pursuing a new position. For example, "Hi, I'm Jane Anderson. I'm a marketing professional with more than ten years of experience in the hotel industry, and I'm currently looking for a new opportunity."

**Where can I find a guide for writing a good résumé and bio?**

We suggest looking at the résumés and bios of people you admire and then using those as a rough guide. Obviously you cannot copy them word for word, but you can follow the format and tone to weave a powerful story about you and your experience.

**What should I consider before writing a blog?**

Writing a blog is a big commitment of time and brain power. You must be ready to post new content at least once a week. Blog readers always want something new, and a blog that has not been updated becomes stale very quickly. Also, consider the topics that you will cover. A blog must have a focus and a theme, and while you can go off topic on occasion, your readers will come back regularly because they care about your message. Having a blog can help position you as an expert, but that won't happen overnight. It can take years to find your audience, so be patient and tenacious.

# 6

# BUILDING RELATIONSHIPS
# THROUGH NETWORKING

As we've discussed, the third step of networking involves relationship building. To establish the trust that is needed in a relationship and to identify opportunities to help one another, you'll need to know more about each other than is found on a business card. This requires a creative and consistent effort of discovery, both immediately after meeting someone new, and once you've established a rapport. Make sure you focus on finding the things that you have in common, and on creating a shared history of experiences, rather than on what you hope to reap from the relationship.

## The process: managing a new relationship

Once you have begun to implement your networking plan, you'll find yourself beginning to meet new people and make important contacts. You might also find yourself asking, "So, now what?" In other words, how do you manage and develop these new relationships so that they can become mutually beneficial? Fortunately, there is a straightforward process that you can follow. This process is meant to be a guide; as with everything in networking, you'll need to make adjustments for your own situation and comfort level.

Let's examine the process for two different scenarios:

## Scenario #1

Tammy is in commercial real estate, and she is having lunch with Mark, an executive recruiter with whom she has a successful referral relationship. During lunch Mark runs into Greg, one of his clients, the CEO of a growing biotech company. He introduces Greg to Tammy, and during the course of their short conversation Greg comments, "We expect to add another 15 or 20 employees by the end of the year. At this rate, we'll need more office space by this time next year!" Here is one follow-up strategy for Tammy:

| TASK | TIMELINE |
|------|----------|
| *Research Greg thoroughly.* Google him. Read his company's website. Ask Mark for his insight. Ask co-workers what they know about the company. Utilize industry sources for additional information. | Prior to contacting Greg |
| *Initiate contact with Greg.* A personal phone call or snail-mailed packet will have more impact than an e-mail. The most important thing is to reach out – somehow! Remind Greg how they met, referring to Mark by name, and directly state specific reason for the contact. Ask for a face-to-face meeting. | Within 2-3 days of the introduction |

| TASK | TIMELINE |
|---|---|
| *Schedule a meeting.* Do this at Greg's office at a date and time convenient for him. | Suggest a date 1-2 weeks out |
| *Confirm meeting.* | 48 hours prior to meeting |
| *Prepare materials.* These are personalized for Greg, demonstrating Tammy's knowledge of his company and industry. Make sure that Tammy's ability to provide a relevant solution is clear. Practice presentation. | Prior to the meeting |
| *Arrive for meeting 5 - 10 minutes early.* Allow some time to build rapport with Greg before launching into the business presentation. | The day of the meeting |
| *Send a personal, hand-written thank-you note.* | Within 48 hours |
| *Send a follow-up letter with any additional information requested during meeting.* | Within one week |
| *Ask for the business.* This can be done subtly (i.e. "I'd appreciate the opportunity to work together") but it must be done. Greg wants to hear that Tammy wants his company's business. | During the meeting, and in all follow-up materials |

## Scenario #2

Julia is the new owner of a small gift shop, and recently attended a regional conference for female business owners. There she meets Annette, who owns and operates a chain of car washes in a city two hours away from Julia. Julia and Annette immediately hit it off, and attend several of the conference's events together. While Julia does not see an immediate opportunity to do business with Annette, she has learned a lot from her new friend, and sees her as a potential mentor. Here is one way Julia can follow up with Annette:

| TASK | TIMELINE |
|---|---|
| *Research Annette.* Read the company's website and Google her. | 24 - 48 hours after returning home |
| *Send Annette a hand-written note.* Julia should tell Annette how much she enjoyed getting to know her at the conference and how she appreciated Annette's advice. Julia may want to include a brochure on her shop. | Within one week |
| *Look for opportunities to visit Annette in her city, or to meet again at another event.* | Ongoing |

| TASK | TIMELINE |
|------|----------|
| *Ask Annette for help on specific business issues or opportunities that present themselves.* Julia should be careful that she is not asking too much from Annette and is reaching out to her only on significant, relevant issues. | Ongoing |
| *Brainstorm on ways Julia could help Annette, personally or professionally, and make this offer.* Julia never knows where she might be of assistance, and simply extending the offer will make a positive impression. | Ongoing |

Having a list of specific tasks with deadlines will help Tammy and Julia (and you!) ensure that networking opportunities do not slip away. It's easy to be enthusiastic in the early stages of building a new relationship, but it's also easy to lose momentum as time goes by. With proper preparation and consistent follow-up, implementing these steps will help you leverage each new contact.

## Tips for a successful one-on-one meeting

One-on-one meetings are the most effective way to build and maintain relationships with important contacts. While you can't focus your entire networking strategy on spending solo time with others, you should view every personal meeting as a precious gift. There are only 24 hours in a day, and any time that someone agrees to sit down with you is golden.

Meetings give you the chance to:

- Spend quality, focused time together without the distractions of larger gatherings
- Learn more about someone and their business, and tell them about you
- Privately address specific topics or explore potential opportunities
- Strengthen your connection and build trust

People who go into networking meetings without a second thought as to their goals are missing an opportunity. While you may not have a specific agenda for every meeting, always have a purpose and a plan so that the meeting is relevant and valuable for you both.

There are four things to keep in mind when attending any kind of meeting:

1. Be prepared

2. Be respectful

3. Be attentive

4. Be focused

Below are some tips for conducting successful meetings:

- **Prepare, prepare, prepare.** Do your research so you can speak intelligently about the company or the person you are meeting. The Internet makes it easy to do basic research, and your knowledge will make a good impression.

- **Meet according to their schedule and offer to go to their location.** Make the meeting as convenient for the other person as possible. If you are the one requesting the meeting, this is proper etiquette. If a person tells you that a certain time is best for them, make it work for you.

- **Arrive on time and leave on schedule.** Time is a precious commodity. The best way to demonstrate your appreciation for the appointment is to arrive and depart on time. Always predetermine the length of the meeting and confirm it when you arrive.

- **Be respectful of their priorities, requests, and comfort zone.** People tend to talk first about the things that are on their mind the most. Let them dwell on that topic, even if it is not what you most want to discuss. Conversely, if they make a request such as, "I'd prefer not to discuss budgets at this point," then honor that.

- **Watch their body language.** You can tell a lot about a person by paying attention to their body language. If they appear distracted or in a hurry, don't dawdle. If, on the other hand, they appear intrigued by a certain topic, stay with it until they're ready to move on. If they become very animated while discussing another aspect of their business, zone in on that.

- **Do more listening than talking.** This can be hard, especially for extroverts. In general, you will get further by listening. Ask open-ended questions to draw people out; this is how you will learn about their priorities and concerns. Asking them questions not only gives you critical information, but also it demonstrates your interest in them and makes them feel important.

- **Combine professional and personal conversations.** You now know that some of the strongest business connections are initiated through personal connections and vice versa. Invest the time to find the things you have in common, and allow the friendship to take root by discovering the other person's interests.

- **Take notes.** This is another way to make your companion feel important. It is thoughtful, however, to ask the other person if they mind you taking a few notes. Your notes will also give you something to refer to regarding next steps.

- **Summarize what you have heard.** A brief run-down of the key points you discussed during your conversation is an effective way to end a meeting. This is especially true if you agreed upon specific action items. Reiterating and clarifying these items before you leave will make follow-up much easier.

- **Ask for what you want.** Be sure you get what you came for. Your goal for the meeting might be to brainstorm on new client sources. It might be to voice your interest in joining the board of an organization. Whatever it is, make sure you do not leave the meeting without making the ask!

- **Confirm next steps.** It is common for two people to leave an upbeat, enjoyable meeting with no idea of what comes next. Sometimes the next step is obvious, such as providing a referral to a colleague, sending a proposal, forwarding information on an event, or arranging a second meeting. In more general "get to know you" meetings, the next step may be unclear, so take the initiative to suggest one, even if it's just to get together again in a month or two.

While many of these tips seem to be most appropriate for sales professionals, they apply to most types of social interaction. More informal meetings can take place over breakfast, lunch, or happy hour, and it may not feel right to whip out your pen and start taking notes. Still, you should use strategic planning and proper etiquette to ensure a good use of time for both you and your companion.

# Gaining confidence and maintaining momentum

As networking becomes more and more a part of your lifestyle, many of these techniques will become more natural for you. And as your comfort level grows, you will also begin to see results.

Some people are impatient to see the tangible results of their networking. Try not to fall into this trap. You have already invested the time to read this far, so realize that with time and effort, your network can be a valuable asset. Keep these points in mind as you build relationships:

**People do business with people they know and like.** While a lot of factors are weighed into a buying decision — price, quality, reliability — all other things being equal, customers will choose the vendor that they have the best feelings about. In a world where more products and services are being commoditized, having the advantage of being well known and well liked is critical.

**Consistent efforts with multiple contacts are the key to success.** The concept is simple: don't put all your eggs in one basket! While you do need to be strategic, strive to network with people in a variety of environments. Networking is an ongoing task, not to be turned on and off like a faucet. Divide your networking time between building and maintaining existing relationships, and creating and developing new ones.

**No one can network for you.** You cannot delegate networking to your marketing manager or business partner. As much as you may see it as a task that you would rather ignore, you are the only one who can build your own reputation and image.

---

**Tracy is a CPA who wants to expand her practice. She believes that her firm is not running enough advertisements on her specialty, medical practices, and that is why she does not have enough business. The firm's marketing manager, Jason, explains to Tracy that advertising is simply a tool to give the firm name recognition and credibility, and while it might help prospective clients find her, she must also network. To supplement the firm's advertising program, Jason suggests that Tracy attend events hosted by their state medical association, and offer to be a guest speaker at a conference for physicians. She could also submit guest articles to this organization's publication, which would highlight her expertise while providing useful information. In order to win more clients in a relationship sales environment, Tracy needs to build credibility and relationships, and for that there are no shortcuts.**

---

You're not just selling a product or service; you're selling a relationship. In today's ultra-competitive environment, relationships are not only important, they are *the* most crucial tool for your ongoing professional success. These relationships will give you the advantage in getting clients and referrals, as well as keeping the ones you have. An established relationship will provide ongoing value beyond your product or service.

**Your network is bigger than you think.** Do you feel like the only people in your network are the ones you know personally? In reality, your network includes not only those people, but also all the people in *their* networks. Likewise, their networks actually include everyone in yours. You just need to let people know what type of contacts you have, and what contacts you are looking to make. A network is healthy when everyone helps each other. Many women do this every day by calling friends to find a good housekeeper or asking their neighbor where she got her son's adorable birthday cake. You may just need to extend this practice to your professional life.

---

**"The best way to build a business relationship is to add real and unique value. Listen well and you'll discover what's really important to people. This is priceless information as it allows you to make a positive and lasting impression by adding a personal touch."**

**Kim Padgett**
**The Padgett Group**
**Houston, Texas**

# The next level of networking

Once you have gotten into your groove and established your own networking strategies, look for new and different ways to make contacts. Consider these:

**Network with your competition.** Instead of viewing your competition as the enemy, consider the reasons you should know them:

*Critical information:* You can be assured that in conversations with clients, prospects, and other influencers, the names of your competitors will come up. It's in your best interest to know them, and their strengths and weaknesses. Knowing your competition takes some of the fear out of competing with them, and will prepare you to respond appropriately. For example, if they are the market leader, if they are offering a new line of products, or if they provide deep discounts, you will know what's coming.

*Potential leads:* It's common in many industries to gain leads from your competitors when they are unable to take on the business themselves. For example, a law firm could be ethically conflicted doing work for a company because of a pre-existing relationship with the adverse party or a competitor. Or the firm might not specialize in the area of law in which the company needs help. It is then in the firm's best interest to refer the company to another firm. In doing so, the attorney makes a good impression with the company by saving them a lot of time and effort in finding the right representation. If future opportunities to work together arise, the company will remember this favor. And, the attorney has strengthened his or her relationship with a competing law firm, which could lead to that firm returning the favor by sending prospects their way.

*Finding talent:* As your own company grows and you need to find new employees, you can tap into your network. If you already know your competition, then you probably know who the superstars are within the industry. You will know who has the right personality, skills, experience, and work ethic to thrive in your organization. This simple networking strategy can make the hunt for key employees much easier, saving you time and money.

*Future employment:* Similarly, it is not uncommon for other companies to look to their competition when opportunities arise within their organization. If you are visible to your competition, and have a good reputation, you could easily make the short list for big career moves.

**Become a Go-To Person.** Having a network makes you more valuable. People turn to you when they need information, not because they think you know everything or everyone, but because they know that you will know where to *find* the answer. Why would you want to be a Go-To Person? You might find it bothersome to frequently have people contact you with random inquiries. In reality, it depends on how you look at it. Is it an effort to answer a call or e-mail, and then think about whom to direct the person to? Of course. But, if one of your goals is to make yourself first in the mind of others in your community, you've succeeded. And you will certainly gain the appreciation, trust, and loyalty of those you've helped.

The trick to being a Go-To Person is not to be selfish. If you know someone who has a need, and you know another who provides that service or product, make the introduction without concern for what you get out of the deal. What goes around comes around. Be mindful, however, about simply providing information, not an actual reference, unless you have personal experience with the person or company you are referring. You may someday be held accountable for the performance of that company, unless you make it clear you are providing an introduction and not making a recommendation.

**Open your network to others.** Once a quarter, look at your contact database and give some thought to those who would benefit from knowing each other. Here are two easy ways to do this:

1. Pick out five people whom you know well and search for those it would be mutually beneficial for them to know.

2. Pick out the five newest additions to your network and search through your database to see whom you can introduce them to.

Either way, make it a habit of linking up people in person, or through an introductory phone call or e-mail. Everyone wins when you do this.

## *Thom Says:*

When I first considered moving to Austin in 1991, a family friend counseled me against it. He was a man of my father's generation who had lived in Austin for two decades and told me that it was not the right move for a young person because the small city was a hard place for an outsider to successfully break into. Since I had not grown up in Austin nor attended the University of Texas, he thought I would never be able to "get networked."

Fortunately he was wrong. I have built a very successful life in my adopted hometown. The reason: I did not shy away from networking. Additionally, the Austin metro area has doubled in size since my arrival, so the business community is now made up of more newcomers than original residents.

The lesson here: never shy away from trying to build a network. Even when you feel like an outsider, don't let it stop you. Everyone is an outsider when they first arrive, but if you take the time to help others, you will slowly gain acceptance. In 2006 and 2007 I was honored to serve as the master of ceremonies for the Austin Chamber of Commerce Awards Dinner, an annual event attended by more than 1,200 people. They were proud moments for a kid who was told he would never be part of the community.

## *Marny Says:*

I frequently tell myself, "You just never know." This helps me keep an open mind when deciding where to spend my networking time. The idea is simply that you just never know where something will go until you give it a try. While we all need to be judicious with our time, it is easy to fall into the trap of only doing those networking activities for which we see a direct or immediate benefit.

For me, as a marketing consultant and professional speaker, it is easy to stick with attending American Marketing Association and National Speaker Association events. Those activities are certainly worthwhile, but taking a chance on something new can also be beneficial.

Consider this unexpected networking opportunity: I was working at a charitable golf tournament when I ran into a former client. We chatted for a while, and it turned out that he was on the board of directors for the charity, and was impressed by the media coverage I had garnered at this function. I sent him a follow-up note and my business card, and he called to ask me to coffee. Prior to the coffee I was fairly sure that he was going to ask for pro bono public relations assistance for his personal cause. Boy was I in for a surprise! Our meeting actually focused on the fact that his company was merging with two other firms, and that the new company was going to need a new brand and a media campaign. Three months later I was hired as project manager for creating and launching the new brand.

The moral of the story? You just never know! So be sure to take a few calculated risks in your networking activities.

# FAQ:

**What are some subtle but effective ways I can ask for business?**

When you network with business professionals, it won't come as a surprise that you want their business or referrals. However, *how* you ask can make all the difference. Be up front; let your contact know that you would welcome the opportunity to work with them or be referred by them to others. Emphasize that you provide quality products and services, and want the chance to earn their business. However, be prepared for them not to immediately jump on board, and do not let their rejection get to you. Many people may already have solid ties with your competitor. Respect their loyalty and continue to develop the friendship, as you never know what tomorrow will bring.

**When I'm networking, does every contact I make have to be for business?**

No. Remember that networking is a lifestyle, not just a sales technique. You want to make real friendship connections in your business community. Some people you meet will lead to business, others will become social friends, and others will just be nice people whom you have met. Treat everyone with respect and try to find ways to help them achieve their goals and you will be rewarded.

**At coffee or lunch, how do I handle that awkward moment when the check
arrives?**

If you invited the other person, you should grab the
check. If you are dining with someone you know well or
meet with often, it is most appropriate to alternate who
pays. Try saying, "I'll get this one, you can get the next
one." Women should not expect male colleagues to pay
simply because they are men; this diminishes their power
as equals.

**How do I invite someone to a meeting that has no specific
purpose other than getting to know them better?**

Make the meeting social in nature; do it over coffee,
lunch, or drinks. Be honest that you simply would like to
spend a little time to get to know more about them and
their business. If you originally made a connection over
something specific, such as a hobby, a mutual friend, or
a profession, remind them of this commonality when
you extend the invitation.

**How do I regain control of a meeting when the other person takes the conversation in a different direction?**

It is important to let the other person talk about their hot buttons — and for you to listen — but you can carefully redirect the conversation to your agenda. When the conversation reaches a natural lull, use the opportunity to restate your purpose for the meeting. As you make your points, be sure to ask questions about the topic to draw them into the discussion.

# ORGANIZATIONS AND EVENTS: KEYS TO NETWORKING SUCCESS

Joining organizations and attending events are two efficient ways to build, expand, and maintain your network. Both should be a part of your networking plan. Organizations give you the opportunity to regularly meet and interact with people, and to connect with people who have similar interests. Ideal organizations offer networking events, educational programs, volunteer and leadership opportunities, and additional resources to members.

Attending events is also an efficient method of networking, due to the sheer number of people who participate. While there are times that a one-on-one meeting is the most appropriate strategy, attending events will bring you in contact with many potential contacts. When your time is constrained, events enable you to meet multiple new people, renew acquaintances, or build relationships, all in an hour or two.

## Choosing the right organizations

There are countless organizations that you can join, regardless of your job function, industry or geography. Do some research to determine which groups are the right fit for you.

Make sure that the groups you are evaluating will help you to attain your networking goals. As with networking, membership is a two-way street. You will need to be able to contribute *to* the organization, as well as benefit *from* it.

As you consider membership, ask yourself:

1. What do I hope to gain from joining this organization?

2. What do I hope to bring to this group?

3. Is this association the *best* use of my time and energy?

4. Will this organization help me achieve my networking goals?

If you can't clearly articulate the answers to these questions, then you may have additional research to do before making the commitment to join.

Here are a few types of organizations to consider:

## Professional Associations

Professional associations focus their membership around a job function, such as accountants or physicians, or a specific industry, such as software or automotive. These organizations range from small, local groups to huge international associations. Many national organizations have local or regional chapters; members benefit both from networking with local peers and from leveraging the resources of a nationwide community. The Financial Executives Institute, the American Marketing Association, and the American Institute of Architects are examples of national organizations with a widespread national presence.

## Business Organizations

Business organizations tend to function on a local or regional level. They often address the needs of an entire local business community, or a particular issue within that community such as transportation infrastructure or workforce retention. Business organizations sometime focus on a particular segment of the business community that crosses industries and professions, such as women or young professionals. Membership in these organizations is especially beneficial as they offer access to a wide variety of professionals and a diversity of events.

A chamber of commerce is one such broad-spectrum business organization. Some cities have women's chambers of commerce that address issues specific to female business owners and leaders. Denver, for example, has a main chamber of commerce, the Denver Metro Chamber of Commerce, as well as a number of chambers that focus on geographic areas within and adjoining the city. Denver also has an active Colorado Women's Chamber of Commerce.

## Community and Social Organizations

Community and social organizations provide local opportunities to participate and serve. Rotary International is one well-known group. Clubs built around a common interest such as reading, running, or scrapbooking can help you build your network. Because people do business with people they know and like, community and social organizations can lead to business relationships.

## Charitable Organizations

Charitable organizations often draw upon local business leaders to volunteer on their boards. If you want to make connections with these people, then roll up your sleeves and dig in. Volunteering for charitable organizations is an excellent way to network with a variety of people within your community, all while serving a worthy cause. However, before you donate your time, be sure that you have a real commitment to the cause. If you are just present to schmooze then your commitment will not be strong enough to get you through the long hours and hard work that are required. Additionally, people can see through a façade, and if you are not honestly interested in the charity, you will not succeed in building genuine relationships.

If you are unsure of how to find a charitable organization that is a good fit for you, go to <u>volunteermatch.org.</u> This website helps would-be volunteers clarify their interests and skills, and then matches them with a local charity in search of assistance.

There is also a unique female organization called the National Charity League. Established in Los Angeles in 1947, NCL offers mothers and daughters the chance to volunteer together in philanthropic and educational opportunities. This mother/daughter volunteer force today works in 196 chapters in 23 states, with more than 55,000 active members. NCL is a great way for busy mothers to give back to their community while setting a good example for their daughters and spending time with them.

---

**Charitable/Community Organizations:**

1) P.E.O. International (Philanthropic Educational Organization) – peointernational.org

2) National Charity League, Inc. – nationalcharityleague.org

3) The Association of Junior Leagues International Inc. – ajli.org

4) American Association of University Women – aauw.org

5) National Organization for Women – now.org

---

## University Alumni Organizations

University alumni groups can be one of the most natural networking experiences, as all members immediately have one thing in common – their alma mater. The same can be said about sorority alumni associations. If you were a member of a sorority in college and have not joined its local alumni group, you are missing a huge networking opportunity! Sorority sisters are more than willing to help each other find jobs or meet new people, and can be a great way to find a mentor. These groups often hold regional or national conferences, which can also offer excellent networking. University and sorority alumni organizations are especially helpful if you have just moved to a new community. Alumni groups often hold social events and organize volunteer projects – and you'll have a leg up in getting involved in your new community.

"When I started the Phoenix office for my company I did not know a soul here. Networking with people became my lifeline. I joined organizations, asked people to introduce me to their connections, connected from those connections and developed relationships. Industries and communities are smaller than you think, even in a big city."

Kelly Bell
BURY
Phoenix, AZ

## Finding the Right Organizations

How can you find the organizations that will enable you to be a contributing, involved member while also providing you with access to relevant people?

1. Ask your peers and mentors. Find out where your industry colleagues and co-workers are involved. Talk to your friends as well, even if they aren't in the same job, stage of life, or city as you. If they can't give you a specific recommendation, they may know someone who can.

2. Search the web and your local newspapers. You may have to play around with searches and review multiple websites to find relevant information, but it is out there and in great quantity.

3. Attend an event and talk to members about what benefits they find from their involvement. See for yourself what attending the organization's events are like, and whether you fit in with the members and share the group's agenda. Ask members how they felt about this program compared to other events they have attended in the past. While speaking to people, be sure to ask what their level of involvement with the organization is, as someone who attends events only occasionally may be less enthusiastic than a committed member.

**Professional Women's Organizations**

1) Executive Women's Forum – ewf.usa.com

2) National Association of Women Business Owners – nawbo.org

3) Women in Technology International – witi.com

4) Accounting & Financial Women's Alliance – afwa.org

5) The Association for Women in Communications – www.womcom.org

6) Women Presidents' Organization – www.womenpresidentsorg.com

7) National Association for Female Executives – www.nafe.com

8) American Business Women's Association – www.abwa.org

## Leveraging your involvement

Remember that organizations are simply a vehicle for you to further develop your knowledge, skills, reputation, and network. Your role in the organization is as important as the organization itself. Just becoming a member will give you few direct benefits; you will get out of it what you put into it. How can you make the most of the time and money you spend on membership?

**Take advantage of the benefits of membership.** Reading a monthly newsletter or scanning the organization's website will not give you much of a ROI. Benefits will vary greatly from organization to organization, ranging from continuing education to health insurance and singles' groups. If the organization offers events or conferences, attend as many as are relevant to you. Regularly reading the organization's newsletter will let you know who the movers and shakers are and give you an idea of whom to seek out while at events.

**Be a leader.** Organizations are rife with members who just pay their dues, attend occasional events, and add the name of the organization to their résumé under "Community Activities." What most organizations really need are volunteer leaders, those members who step up and do the work required to keep the group functioning. Volunteer for committees, including the non-glamorous roles like staffing the sign-in table at events or taking minutes at board meetings. Serving on committees gives you access to leaders, and enables you to build your skills and experience. If, for example, you want to gain more confidence in sales, fund-raising would be a good choice for you.

**Brandy was an active member of her local chapter of the American Society of Interior Designers. When she was asked to join the executive board as treasurer, she was terrified. She wanted to serve the group, but since she was not an accountant she did not feel qualified for the role. However, she wanted to help, and reluctantly took on the task. Upon the completion of her year as treasurer, she found that her fear of math was much worse than her actual skills at it. She was able to improve the group's financial status, and the next year she was asked to be vice president. Additionally, when she opened her own business two years later, she was not as intimidated by the financial aspects that were required of her as an entrepreneur.**

**Work the roster.** Without a doubt, the single biggest advantage to joining an organization is your fellow members. They will be a resource for ideas, contacts, advice, and camaraderie. Within the membership ranks are referral sources, clients, friends, partners, mentors, and future employees. It is relatively easy to build relationships with other members since you will interact regularly. Be careful not to cross the line from networking into sales, however, as it may make other members uncomfortable. Many groups have rules against soliciting the membership for your own business purposes. However, once you have made a connection with someone, use your best judgment on how to discuss your company or service. Most people are willing to listen to business presentations from people they know, but they might resent your assuming that just because you are a member of the same group you can call them. Get to know people first.

**Know when to move on.** Not every organization is appropriate for lifetime membership. People change careers, get promoted, move to new cities, and develop new interests. When these changes occur, networking goals often change, as well. Don't be afraid to move on to new organizations and away from associations that no longer are a fit for you. It may be hard to let go, especially if you have served in a leadership role and have long-standing friendships within the group. If you are serving on the board, limit your service to three years on the executive committee. You do not want to become the person who begins each meeting with a history lesson of how the board acted seven years earlier. If the organization is still a good fit for you to remain involved, drop off of the board and give others an opportunity.

# Making the most of events

When most people think about a networking event, they envision a crowd milling around a hotel banquet room with cocktails in one hand and business cards in the other. However, there are almost as many types of networking events as there are networking organizations. Events range from breakfast meetings with a dozen people, to speaker luncheons with 100 attendees, to black tie dinners with more than 1,000. Each can be a valuable experience if you make the most of the opportunity.

As with joining organizations, attending events is only an effective use of your time and money if you do so with a plan. Ask yourself, "What do I hope to gain from attending?" The more tangible your answer is, the more likely you are to see results. For example, if you are a member of the organization that is hosting the event, your goal may be to network with other members. Perhaps the event is featuring a guest speaker on a topic that is interesting to you personally. Or, the event might offer you access to a particular group of people that you would like to meet. The important thing is to attend with that benefit firmly in mind.

If you are not sure why you are going to an event, or how you hope to benefit, or if your heart just isn't in it, your time is better spent elsewhere. Many people show up to events late, sit by themselves, speak only to people they know, and then sneak out early. This is an example of what *not* to do. These people go home thinking, "Well, that event was a waste of time," when actually it was a wasted opportunity.

There are several strategies you can use to ensure that attending an event is a good investment:

**Research the event or host prior to attending.** When attending an event, you want to be knowledgeable about both the event and the host. The Internet makes this simple. This information will make it easier for you to engage in conversation, so take a few moments to become familiar with the host organization, the guest speaker and topic, or the criteria for an awards program.

**Attend with a colleague.** There are several advantages to attending an event with a colleague, the least of which is that you are not on your own. If you are new to networking or are an introvert, it can be especially comforting to know that someone is right there with you. They can give you a landing point if you find yourself wandering the room alone or in between conversations. Attending with a colleague also gives you twice as many opportunities to meet people because you can meet the people your colleague already knows.

**Invite clients, prospects, and referral sources to attend with you.** Events are an easy way to utilize your multi-tasking skills. If you are planning to attend an event, ask yourself which of your clients, prospective clients, or key referral sources might be interested in attending as well. This can be an extraordinarily good use of your time – not only will you be spending time networking, you'll also be with someone important to your business. It's nice if you can pay for them, but if not, it is still okay to invite them along. Just make sure that they are aware of the cost so that you do not end up with an awkward situation.

**Arrive early for the best networking.** There is no question that the best networking is at the beginning of an event – regardless of whether the event is in the morning, at lunch, or in the evening. Attendees will be in a rush to get to the office or go home as soon as the event is over, so if you are hoping to connect with someone, do it first thing. Since many events feature a speaker or program that will limit your time to network, arrive early to interact with other attendees before taking a seat. Also, upon arriving, you can scan the table of pre-printed name tags to see who will be there. It is also easier to walk into a nearly empty room than it is to try to join 200 people who are already engaged in discussion. When you arrive early, it is as if the others join your party instead of you struggling to get up to speed.

**Spend your time both initiating new relationships *and* building existing ones.** It is easy to arrive at an event, see a friend or professional contact, and spend your time catching up with them. But you must also commit to meeting new people and initiating new relationships, even though this can be a bit more intimidating. Aim to meet three to five new people at each event. If you keep this goal in mind, you will be conscious of the time you spend talking with any one person.

**Use strategic seating.** When events feature a speaker or program, keep in mind that your networking does not have to stop when you take your seat. People tend to sit with people they already know. Instead, try sitting next to someone you haven't met. There will probably be a few minutes to chat with your tablemates prior to the start of the program, so make good use of this time. Be sure to exchange business cards before you leave the table. You can also purchase or reserve tables at key events, and invite people to either attend as your guest or reimburse you for seats at your table.

**Follow up within three days of an event.** Follow-up is the most neglected aspect of networking, even though it is also the most important. We've all met someone at an event, had a good conversation and made a connection, exchanged business cards, meant to schedule a follow-up meeting or send them information, then somehow let it slip through the cracks. Prompt follow-up can make or break a new relationship. Make it a priority and a habit.

# Event etiquette

There is quite a bit of etiquette involved in attending events, and yes, people *do* notice. You want to come across as professional, polished, and confident. Here's a refresher:

**Be prepared to introduce yourself, colleagues, and guests.** The most common error people make while at events involves introductions. People either don't introduce themselves or don't introduce the people that they are with. This creates an awkward moment. It is especially common when a group of people in conversation are joined by someone new. It is proper etiquette to introduce the newcomer to everyone in the group as soon as they join you. Try to include first and last names, their company or profession (if appropriate), and an idea of how you know each other. An example of this type of introduction is:

> *"Greg, I'd like you to meet Sally Fielding, a partner at the accounting firm of Jackson, Willis & Summers. Sally, this is Greg Walters, a freelance graphic designer I've worked with on many projects."*

**Respect quiet time.** When a networking event has moved into a meeting with a program or a guest speaker, it's time to be quiet, regardless of how engaged you are in conversation. Respect the speaker by paying attention. If someone tries to engage you in conversation at an inappropriate time, smile, nod, and then break eye contact, returning your attention to the speaker. If your colleague persists, you may have to tell him or her (quietly and respectfully, of course) that you would like to listen to the speaker. Good manners and respectful behavior are always noticed, as are their negative counterparts.

**Silence your phone.** These devices have been a great help to networking in many ways, but they have also created some etiquette challenges. Whether you are in a one-on-one meeting, mingling at an event, or listening to a panel of experts, there is no acceptable time to answer a call or read/send a text message unless it is a true emergency. By doing so, you are telling the people you are with that they are not as important as you or the call/text/email that has diverted your attention. Many people have fallen into the habit of utilizing these tools anytime, anywhere. If you catch yourself doing it, stop!

**Be inclusive, attentive, and interested.**

Are you an Excluder? At events there are often small, tight groups of people that seem impenetrable, and may intimidate you so much that you won't approach them. They may actually be reminiscent of high school cliques! Strive to be the opposite, including and welcoming people into your conversations. Networking is, by definition, an inclusive activity, and events are a perfect place to expand your circle of contacts.

Are you a Scanner? There are also people who constantly scan the room, looking to see who else is there. While you might think this is a good networking practice, it is actually rude if you do it while talking to someone. It gives them the impression that you are looking for someone better to talk to, and may also leave them feeling like you're not listening to them. Focus on the person you are talking to, and you'll both get more from the interaction.

Are you an Egomaniac? Do you monopolize the conversation? It's easy to dominate conversations without even being aware of it, so check yourself. If you need to divert the focus to someone else, or need to restart a conversation that may have hit a natural lull, try a few of these questions:

1. What do you do?

2. What does your company do?

3. What are your biggest current challenges in your job/company/industry?

4. What is the best part of your job?

5. How are you connected to (name of organization hosting the event)?

6. Are you involved with any organizations or charitable causes?

Always RSVP, arrive on time, and leave early only with great discretion. Again, this boils down to respecting the event's host and attendees. RSVPs are critical as they enable the event's organizers to plan for the appropriate amount of food, beverages, seats, name tags, etc. It will reflect badly on you if you do not RSVP but show up anyway, just as it will if you RSVP but do not attend. Arriving on time is the most professional thing to do, while arriving late will draw unwelcome attention to you. If you must leave an event early, slip out discreetly at an appropriate time, such as between speakers or when the wait staff is clearing dishes. And, of course, bid your tablemates farewell as you depart, letting them know why you must leave early lest they think they have driven you away. Whatever you do, DO NOT try and sneak out by crouching down in a "walk of shame" as many women do. Simply stand up straight and walk directly and confidently to the exit.

## Seminars and conferences

Seminars and conferences are worth a close look as part of your networking plan. Most organizations have at least one annual conference, and many have regional conferences throughout the year. Some organizations offer events specifically for their female members, focusing on issues women face and providing the opportunity for women in the same industry to network with one another. While you should not limit yourself to attending only women-focused events, you should take advantage of them when possible. Women have such few exclusive opportunities to bond in a business setting that you need to grab the chance when it presents itself.

Most conferences have costs associated with them, and some may even involve travel, so you'll need to plan ahead. In addition, there are many single-day seminars that provide an intensive way to evolve your skill set. It is worth noting that you do not necessarily have to be a member of an organization to attend their conference or seminar, though there may be a higher cost for non-members.

Most colleges and universities offer continuing education programs. Some are even accompanied by a certification. These programs may provide opportunities to meet successful, key individuals in the local business community who serve as adjunct professors or participate as guest lecturers. Active participation in the class is a way to meet peers and establish rapport with the instructor, which may translate into a future business friendship.

People often do not participate in conferences, claiming that they cannot be out of the office for any period of time, or that they do not believe these events provide enough value to justify their cost. The former is just an excuse for people who are uncomfortable with the networking that goes along with conference attendance. As for the latter, any time you can be in a room full of people with similar careers and interests, you should find a way to be there. You never know whom you might meet. Remember that conferences are not just a venue for meeting potential clients, but also for meeting potential referral sources, vendors, employees, employers, and partners.

Still, you must do more than show up; you need to make an effort to meet and get to know people. Use the non-classroom time to your benefit; networking can be done at lunch, dinner, and on coffee breaks. If there is a bar in the hotel lobby, this is a good place to meet other attendees. Conferences and seminars are a great place to practice the tips provided earlier in this chapter.

## Visibility vs. credibility

One of the perks that comes with active participation in organizations and events is raising your visibility. There are also pitfalls if you do not act appropriately. Anyone can be visible – if you are in enough places often enough, people will begin to recognize you, and your name will become known. Being credible, however, is a higher level of recognition where your expertise, integrity, and influence develop into a positive reputation. In short, your personal brand.

How can you create the right kind of visibility while developing credibility?

**Participate only in relevant organizations and events.** Focus your participation on things that make sense for your business and personal interests, rather than simply trying to be in as many places as possible. You don't want people trying to figure out why a travel agent is attending a meeting of dental hygienists.

**Follow through with your commitments.** If you take on any kind of a volunteer role, be sure to deliver what you promised. The quickest way to develop a negative reputation is to fail to follow through. Only commit to those activities you know you have the time and ability to accomplish. Following through is equally important when offering to help people, whether by introducing them to a potential client, helping them find a job, or passing on the contact information of a great babysitter. People *will* remember whether you kept your word.

**Develop relationships, not contacts.** This is a classic case of quantity versus quality. If a large number of people have heard of you and perhaps even met you once or twice, this constitutes visibility. If a smaller number of people personally know you, can speak to your unique capabilities, and will serve as an advocate for you, this constitutes credibility. Focus on developing relationships and trust with key individuals, within key organizations, and at key events, rather than using mass marketing techniques.

---

**Nadine was a financial planner who relied on networking to gain referrals and clients. She was an avid networker, attending as many events as possible each week. She worked the crowd and passed out a flurry of business cards. She joined multiple organizations, and pursued volunteer leadership roles on several committees and boards. Nadine's active participation and consistent presence quickly gained her visibility, and her name was soon well known within the business community. Her follow-through, however, was less enthusiastic, and her work behind the scenes was inconsistent and ineffectual. Just as quickly, she gained a reputation as being unreliable and a taker, and people began to wonder how she fit work in with all of her networking activities. While she continued to participate in events, Nadine lost credibility, and faced an uphill battle to regain a good reputation.**

---

**And then there is Janie. Shortly after Janie moved to town, she began to meet people in the local business community. She cautiously asked people about the important organizations for young entrepreneurial professionals. She never abused any confidences and slowly began to make friends. She volunteered with a local charity and became one of its board members. A year after her arrival, Janie decided to start her own catering business. She had a track record of successes and had developed a good reputation, so it was easy for her to partner with other companies and quickly bring on customers. While she was building the new company, she continued to network, make introductions, and volunteer. She now employs more than a dozen full-time people and has received numerous business and civic awards. She knows many important people in town and is regularly sought after for her counsel. Janie is both visible and credible.**

Many people become well known and well liked, but that alone will not get them much, and eventually people will see through the façade. To be famous without substance is basically useless, both personally and professionally. Experience, ethics, hard work, and commitment provide credibility, which is of real value.

## *Thom Says:*

I discovered that if you are consistent in your networking, people will eventually accept you. When I first began building my network I was constantly worried that I was not smart enough or did not have the right experience to attend many industry events. However, I found that over time, all those shortcomings were just in my head. Most people I met were interested in getting to know me as much as I was interested in meeting them.

After years of participating in the business community, I never second-guess whether I belong at an event. I am comfortable in my own skin and in my successes, and do not worry about what others might think. I believe this makes me appear more confident, and thus more approachable in group settings.

Be patient and persistent in your networking and you will fit in.

## Marny Says:

At one point during my career, I found myself somewhat unexpectedly at a crossroads in my networking plan. I was a partner in a successful marketing communications firm, in a city that was growing by leaps and bounds. I had ten years of real-world experience and had built both a solid reputation and a fantastic network. I had close friends, mentors, happy clients, and happy employees. I was engaged to be married and buying my first house. I traveled at least one day a week for work, and was chairing the board of directors of the largest theatre in our city. I had achieved almost all of these milestones (including meeting my husband-to-be) by steady, strategic networking. But I was also burning out.

One day I attended networking functions at breakfast, lunch, and happy hour. As I looked across the patio of a trendy bar that evening, at a private reception for an equally trendy venture capital firm, I noticed at least a dozen people whom I had seen at one of the networking events I had attended earlier that day. This was an eye-opener and also a wake up call! I realized I was over-networking. Quality had turned into quantity, and I needed to cut back.

It was a relief, actually, as I set limits on the number of functions I would attend in a week. It was difficult to turn down invitations at first, and I had more than a few anxious moments when I'd hear about a great event that I missed. But I soon realized that I could focus more time maintaining the relationships I'd spent the last decade building. Over the next few months, I revised my networking plan to be more strategic and to reflect the changes in my life, both personally and professionally.

# FAQ:

**What kind of time commitment is involved in serving on the board of a professional organization?**

This will vary with each organization; however, you should expect at least one board meeting and one additional committee meeting each month. As a board member, you will also be expected to attend the organization's events regularly, and to represent the organization at other functions in your community. There will also be work outside of meetings and events, often including raising funds. Find out the expectations of board members *before* you make the decision.

**Should I pay for my membership or should my employer?**

If the organization is directly related to your profession or industry, your employer should support your membership. Forward-thinking companies recognize the value of having their employees involved in the community and will also pay dues for community or charitable organizations.

**How do I politely disengage from someone that I've been talking to at an event?**

Break eye contact and then locate someone across the room that you want to talk to. Then simply say, "It was so great talking to you. Please excuse me, I see a colleague I need to talk to." You can also try giving them your business card and asking for their card – a commonly understood signal to end a conversation.

**How do I join a group of people talking at a networking event?**

The more confidence you have in approaching a group, the more successful you will be. If you know someone in the group, make eye contact with them and say, "Hi, Kevin, how are you?" If it's a group of strangers, make eye contact with one and introduce yourself. Do not hover on the edge of the group and, if they seem to be engaged in a serious private discussion, do not intrude.

**What do I do if I can't remember someone's name?**

There will be times when you run into someone whom you have met before and you will blank out on his or her name. This is just part of being human. When this happens, just own up to it quickly. Tell the person that you know you have met before, but you are sorry you cannot recall their name. Most people will understand that these things happen, and will not hold it against you (unless you forget their name again and again each time you see them).

Another way to overcome this is to introduce the person to someone else. Ask if they know each other and then pause so they can introduce themselves.

# THE MANY FACES OF NETWORKING

As you know, networking takes many forms and serves many purposes. While it takes consistent effort and creativity to truly reap the benefits of networking, it also can become a comfortable, natural part of your professional life. In order to build mutually beneficial relationships, it is crucial to keep an open mind and opportunistic attitude. And remember, you're probably networking even when you don't realize it!

## Creativity counts

It is easy to follow the leader. You frequently see this in marketing; companies advertise where their competitors advertise, assuming that it works well for the other company. It's a better strategy to stand apart, however, even though it often takes more time, energy, and resources. After all, new and unusual ideas get more attention.

Consider holiday cards. How many of the cards that you received last year had laser-printed labels and lacked a personal signature? The computer has been a great productivity-enhancing tool, but a foil-stamped signature and an Avery® label is hardly a warm and fuzzy greeting of the season. We're not suggesting that you stop sending holiday cards or abandon common seasonal activities because frankly, it's even worse to be noticed by your absence. Instead, expand your activities beyond the predictable.

Here are some examples of adding creativity to your standard networking:

- The owner of a photography studio has joined the board of Habitat for Humanity in her community, and offers to host a board meeting at her offices. Knowing these evening meetings often last several hours, she also springs for a nice selection of wine and appetizers.

- On Mother's Day, a pharmaceutical sales manager sends cards to the female customers and colleagues that she knows have children. She notes that she is a working mom, too, and acknowledges the juggling act they pull off every day.

- A recruiter wants to reconnect with a colleague she hasn't spoken to in several months. Rather than sending an e-mail and inviting the colleague to coffee, she searches the web for a new article on a topic her colleague is interested in and sends that along with a note.

These thoughtful strategies will draw more attention than will more typical approaches.

Hosting creative events is a great way to have personal interaction with clients, potential clients, referral sources and other key influencers. But you have to give people a compelling reason to attend. Here are examples of creative hooks:

- Hosting a grand opening at your new offices

- Introducing your new CEO to customers, partners, and the media

- Featuring the chef at the hottest new restaurant in town at a private tasting menu event

- Collecting back-to-school supplies for low-income children in your community

- Having a well-known and slightly controversial expert in your industry as a guest speaker

There are many types of events that can be effective ways to network with your target market, including easy-to-coordinate informal and inexpensive options.

*Small Gatherings:* When it comes to networking, bigger events are not necessarily better. Gathering with small groups of strategically selected people is a good use of your networking time and dollars. If, for example, you and five colleagues each bring one new person to a lunch, you meet and spend time with five new people – certainly a networking success. Two complementary businesses (such as a commercial architecture firm and a real estate development firm) might also host an event for their clients. While their clients get to meet one another, the two businesses also get to meet potential clients.

*Sporting Events:* One of the most traditional and effective ways to bond with other business people is through sports. On any given day there is a business, charitable, or social golf tournament where new contacts are made, friendships are strengthened, and deals are struck. Golf has long been a staple of client entertaining because people who enjoy golf are thrilled to get out of the office to play. The fact that it is a scenic, quiet game played over the course of several hours lends itself to conversation. Most people that play golf truly love the game, and that in itself can lead to a strong connection between players as they discuss courses, equipment, and handicaps. Most golfers today are men, and in the business world that puts them at a networking advantage. The lesson here? Sisters, it's time to pick up those clubs! It could be one of the best networking moves you ever make.

Larger companies may also have tickets or luxury box suites for their local university or professional sports teams. If used correctly, these can have great impact. If you have access to these types of tickets, think long and hard about how you use them. Attending a game *with* someone is much more beneficial to your relationship than giving them the tickets as a gift. Don't fall into the trap of inviting the same people, time after time. And if you are asked to attend a sporting event with a business colleague, think twice before turning it down, even if you don't enjoy the sport. You will be sharing in the experience with your host, which is valuable. Sporting events generally last about three hours, and much of that time is spent socializing. You may even discover you like a sport once you have been exposed to it a few times.

*Piggy Back Events:* This strategy allows you to leverage other events to ensure attendance at your event, "piggy backing" one onto the other. For example, if there is a cocktail party honoring a retiring community leader from 6:00 – 8:00 p.m., this is a great opportunity to plan a dinner at a nearby restaurant starting at 8:30 pm. Call ahead of time and invite some guests who you know will be at the main event. That way they will know in advance that they will be out later. Also, they will inevitably tell others that they were invited to dinner with you, which is good for your brand awareness and reputation. Save a couple of seats for people you meet at the event. The piggy back strategy also works well when attending industry conferences and trade shows. Check the schedule in advance to see if there is a night when there is no official event planned, and coordinate a small dinner with selected attendees. Or, reserve a suite in the hotel in which the conference is being held, and host a gathering prior to a speaker dinner.

You can make an event memorable by including a unique or unexpected twist, a thoughtful and strategic guest list, or a truly personal touch. Consider the imaginative networking ideas below, and try to incorporate creativity into your own functions:

- Dana frequently entertains clients at dinner, and has developed a trademark dining style. She asks the waiter to serve two of the restaurant's signature desserts as the appetizer – a fun, surprising touch that is appreciated by her guests. Life is short; eat dessert first!

- Each summer, Ellen invites her firm's clients, prospects, and key referral sources to bring their spouses and children to a private Sunday afternoon screening of a new animated feature.

- Kevin and Donna are business partners and sponsors of their local theatre group. They host a customer event that is a dress rehearsal of an upcoming performance, followed by a cocktail party with the actors and director.

- Charlene organizes a team to walk for her local Juvenile Diabetes Research Foundation 5K fundraiser, inviting strategic partners, vendors, and clients to participate. She even creates a team t-shirt featuring the logos of all participating companies.

## Finding a job through networking

People often embrace active networking the most when they are looking for a job. There's nothing like a pink slip to spur someone to crack open their contact database, schedule meetings with colleagues, and attend industry events. Suddenly, they are everywhere. This isn't surprising since networking is by far the best way to find your next job. Consider the following situation:

> Two months ago Carrie was laid off from a large computer manufacturer that made significant staffing cuts. She is not having any luck finding new employment and, in fact, she doesn't even have any prospects. Many of her co-workers have already settled into new positions, despite a slow job market, and it seems that most of them found their opportunities through someone they knew.

> Carrie doesn't believe in networking. She was a workaholic, convinced that if she worked hard she would remain employed. She was wrong. Now that she needs a job, Carrie finds herself behind candidates who had connections. A friend suggested she meet with a well-respected political consultant with clients in the tech industry, to seek advice and contacts. Here's what happened:

1. Carrie asked Joe to meet for coffee. When the check came, Carrie expected Joe to cover it since he had a job.

   *If you invite someone to coffee, lunch, or drinks, you should expect to pay the bill. If the person offers to pay, you can decide if it's appropriate but do not assume that because you are out of work, your guest should buy. You also should never assume that because you are a woman that a male colleague will pay the bill.*

2. Carrie assumed that Joe would bring his address book of contacts for her to utilize in her job search.

   *If you do meet someone with a large network, be respectful that it is their network (not yours) and do not expect them to introduce you to important people that they know. Most people will not risk their reputation to help someone they have just met; remember that it will take time for people to open their network to you.*

3. Carrie was not grateful for Joe's time. Although Joe spent an hour listening to Carrie and offering suggestions, Carrie never said thank you. She figured that because Joe was an active networker, it was no big deal.

   *Be thankful (very thankful!) for anyone who talks with you about your quest. People are more likely to help someone who is genuinely appreciative than someone who simply expects others to help. Even if you don't think that you gained anything from a meeting, be grateful that someone gave you the gift of their time and experience.*

4. Carrie did not follow up with Joe after the meeting. Joe never heard whether Carrie followed any of his suggestions, nor did Carrie tell him when or where she accepted a new position.

   *You should not only thank someone for his or her time and advice, but also keep them apprised of your job search. If you do utilize their advice or contact individuals or companies they recommended, let them know. And when you do find a new job, be sure to give them your new contact information, and thank them again for helping you through your transition.*

If you only network when you're looking for a new career opportunity, people will see through this. As you know from reading this book, networking is a way of life, not a sporadic strategy for when you have a specific or urgent need. If you have taken the time to build your network and your personal brand before you need them, they will be tremendous assets when you do.

"Networking isn't something to do when you're ready for a job change, it's something you do every day. My networks inside and outside my work have helped shape my career. I am always open to meeting and learning from new people. That is the only way I have successfully evolved my career in a male-dominated industry with little to no fear."

**Haley Curry**
**South Texas Energy & Economic Roundtable**
**San Antonio, TX**

# Networking in a male-dominated environment

Women who work in male-dominated environments can find networking even more challenging. This can be an intimidating and isolating situation, and is more common than you might think despite the approximately 70 million working female Americans (38% of whom are in professional occupations).[2] Babson College, for example, announced that their research showed that only 6% of all venture capitalist firm partners were women in 2013. Consider these circumstances:

- Mia is a project manager for a commercial construction company.

- Juanita is a sports reporter for a large daily newspaper.

---

[2]  Source – 2006 Catalyst Census

- Jennifer is an operations supervisor in an oil refinery.

For these women, and many others like them, building successful relationships with their peers can be more difficult. Women may be ostracized, patronized, or simply overlooked by male colleagues who believe that their company or industry is no place for a woman. Some men may be overtly rude and confrontational, while others may just be uncomfortable having a woman in their work environment and avoid interaction altogether. Most men simply don't realize what a challenging situation it is for us to be the only woman at a meeting, on a trip, in a team, etc. Whether dealing with male managers, employees, or peers, being the only woman (or one of a very few) can be very lonely indeed.

Women can find themselves working within a male-dominated environment for a variety of reasons. For example, there is no denying that top management positions within Fortune 500 companies are still held mostly by men; in 2014 women held just 14.6% of corporate officer positions.[3] But other factors can lead to this as well. It seems that men gravitate toward certain professions (engineers, stock brokers, pilots) more than women do. Even within professions where women are well represented, there are still specialties that are dominated by men. For example, while women account for about half of all physicians, the specialties of orthopedics and neurosurgery are predominantly male and only 15.9% of medical school

---

[3]  Source – 2006 Catalyst.com Census

deans are women. Acknowledging this doesn't really make it any easier for the women who face these situations.

If you do work in a primarily male environment and are trying to proactively network, how can you overcome this challenge?

**Use your skills and abilities.** Instead of trying to blend in with the guys, leverage your innate differences. Add the personal touch by asking your male peers about their families, their vacations, and their hobbies. Use your social skills to shine at networking events. Utilize follow-up tools. Follow your intuition to pursue positive people and opportunities.

**Relate to your male colleagues.** Connect with your male co-workers on both a professional and personal level. You will have things in common; you just have to find them. Even if you do not share their interests, if you can engage in conversation with them you will find it easier to network. Take the time to learn a little about a few of these areas, and be prepared to join in the "guy talk." Also, seek their insight and concerns regarding your profession, industry, and company. These topics bridge the gender gap and can help you build rapport.

**Reach out to the other women in your situation.** There is great power in uniting with your sisters ... especially when there are so few of you! Your female colleagues should become a resource in a male-dominated environment. After all, no one knows better than they what you are going through. Not every female co-worker will be your friend simply because you share a gender, but you will find an ally here and there. Women tend to look out for one another – especially when they are a significant minority. But you have to have a real relationship in order to reap these benefits.

**Identify supportive male colleagues and focus on them.** Most men are perfectly comfortable working with women. Instead of worrying about how to handle the occasional one who isn't, focus on building relationships with the good guys. It'll be obvious who they are. These men will include you in conversations, decisions, and opportunities, and will be assets in your network. Additionally, some men develop a fatherly relationship with younger colleagues, serving as valuable mentors and champions. These men can be a great resource, as they can be well connected and will happily open their networks. So, while you will encounter some men who are not evolved, don't let those guys sour you on networking.

**Broaden your networking world.** In order to meet and build relationships with other women, you may need to expand your networking to a regional or national level, or online. While it may seem that there is not another woman alive who is dealing with a similar situation, there are plenty – just maybe not in your zip code. Many organizations have been created to enable women in the same field to meet and share experiences across geographic boundaries. Even if such organizations do not have a chapter close to you, they may hold conferences webinars and TechCasts that allow women from across the country to network. Women in Technology International (WITI) and the American Woman's Society of Certified Public Accountants (AWSCPA) are two such groups.

As with all networking, it will take time for these techniques to pay off, but you *can* succeed even in a challenging environment.

## Networking with an open mind

One of the best things about networking is the wide variety of people you will meet. You will network with people of different genders, lifestyles, generations, cultures and personalities. You'll encounter them in diverse venues, and build relationships in different ways. Even if it's more comfortable to spend time with people just like you, the contacts that can help you achieve your networking goals may be, in fact, quite different.

Differences can occur between generations just as easily as they occur between cultures. The key is to keep your mind open and be respectful while learning to connect with different types of people. Focus on the commonalities that will lead toward your desired results.

---

Diane has been in the landscape design business for 20 years, and she and her partner have decided to grow the firm beyond their three long-time employees. During the process of interviewing junior-level designers, she is surprised by the requested starting salary of these professionals. She is also put off by how many of them asked her about flex time, bonuses for bringing on new clients, and becoming an equity partner in the firm. Diane expressed her displeasure to her partner saying, "I can't believe the expectations these women have. What happened to proving your worth and paying your dues?"

As hard as it may be to for Diane to accept, today's employees have different expectations. We work in an age where flexible schedules, performance-based compensation, and a defined partner track are quite common. While it's true that previous generations did pay their dues, they should also take pride in how far women in business have come. Because of these changes, young women are more confident in business settings than in past generations, and are more comfortable asking for what they want. Diane should not hold this against the designers she is interviewing, or she may miss the chance to hire an outstanding employee and gain access to a new generation of clientele.

It is easy to see the differences as The Continental Divide. In fact, some of the most successful and enjoyable relationships form between people who are from vastly different backgrounds or who are in different stages of life. One of the best ways to grow is by learning from those whose experiences and viewpoints are unlike your own. Consider networking an opportunity to meet and learn from a wide range of interesting people.

## Thom Says:

Many of my clients have young children, and their schedules can make networking difficult. One spring I bought a block of tickets to a baseball game and invited along some of my clients and prospects and their four-year-olds. My daughter and I hosted the evening at the ballpark. For most of the kids, it was their first baseball game. For the dads, it was a chance to mix networking and parenting, something they had not likely done before. It was a fun evening for everyone, and a chance for me to stand out. One guest even pointed out that in all his years of business, he'd had plenty of chances to invite his wife to attend events with him, but never before had he been invited to bring his son.

## Marny Says:

As my career and experience evolved, I found myself in my forties without a solid women's networking organization. I had outgrown many of the groups I had been involved with earlier in my career, and I missed having that sort of sisterhood. I talked with a good friend of mine and we agreed to begin an exclusive gathering of carefully selected women we personally knew. We only wanted other experienced, successful, positive women to participate  and we only wanted to include those who would be open, giving and committed. After our first few meetings, these ladies have each invited one other woman that fits with our mission and our style. We are still in the beginning phases, but so far the resulting group has been fantastic. As a result, I am now able to spend quality time with like-minded women in an intimate environment while making important connections.

# FAQ:

**Should I learn to golf?**

It can't hurt. If you're in an industry where golf is common form of client entertaining, it can certainly be an advantage to learn. Similarly, if you're in an industry where client entertaining happens to center around fly fishing, consider that. Many women have learned to play golf and enjoy the sport. However, if you are not good at the game, or do not want to learn, then just accept the fact that this is not going to be your arena to network and commit to finding another way.

**What do I do if my industry organizations do not have events or programs for women?**

Consider starting one! Just because there isn't one doesn't mean there shouldn't be. Get together with other female members of the group (in person, by conference call or online) and discuss the type of programs that would benefit you. Put together a plan and put it before the powers that be.

**I am looking for a job in an industry I have no experience in; can I attend industry events even if I'm not currently employed within that industry?**

Absolutely, assuming that the events are not limited to just members. If you can attend events as a guest of someone who is currently involved, you will have more credibility and will probably feel more comfortable. As you meet people, be honest about your current position and your interest in joining their field.

**How do you host creative, memorable events with a limited budget?**

Use your creativity to come up with affordable but unusual venues, invitations, and gifts. Fun approaches, like hosting a coffee and donuts celebration for colleagues on the day the kids go back to school, don't cost much but are sure to capture attention. And remember that little things, like printing table place cards and sending personalized thank you notes, can take an event to a whole new level.

**I feel like I network with the same kind of people I work with. How can I meet a wider variety of people?**

Join new organizations or attend different events. Many people feel stuck when their networking is limited to professional organizations, where they meet people just like themselves. Try getting involved with a charitable cause or community organization you are interested in; you are sure to meet many new people through activities like these.

# 9

# NETWORKING WITH MENTORS AND PEER GROUPS

The Road of Life is a bumpy one, filled with both obstacles and opportunities. If you are fortunate enough to instinctively know which way to turn at every fork in the road, and if everyone you meet provides you with excellent advice, then you are very lucky. For the rest of us, it is helpful to have some special people we can turn to for guidance and, on occasion, tough love. Many people find it difficult to ask for help, but having a support team is crucial. It is especially valuable to have these people early in your career and when making major life changes. Whether they are mentors or peer groups, these people can be an important part of your long-term success, and can help you minimize or even avoid many of the hazards that will come along the way. Keep in mind, however, that as in all networking relationships, mentors and peer groups are give-and-take partnerships. Be sure that you offer to help as often as you ask for it.

## What is a mentor?

A good definition of mentor is a wise and trusted teacher or counselor. Anyone with more experience than you can be your mentor. He or she can be older or younger than you, as long as they have more professional or industry knowledge. The relationship can be a formal one where you have scheduled meetings with specific agendas. Or the relationship can be so informal that neither of you even realizes that the person is your mentor. Ideally, you should have multiple mentors that bring a different perspective or expertise, so that no matter what your issue, you have someone with relevant experience to turn to.

A mentor is different from a role model, as a mentor is not only someone who inspires you, but also is accessible and can actively help you. Oprah may be a role model for thousands upon thousands of women, but she is probably only a true mentor to a few. Your mentor is someone whom you regularly turn to for advice, someone who has taken a visible interest in assisting you along the path of your career.

Understanding a Mentor's Role:

- To share their experience, insight, perspective & expertise

- To help you avoid problems & gain access to opportunities

- To help you develop skills & tools

- To provide constructive criticism – don't take it personally!

- To introduce you to their network

Mentors Are NOT:

- Employment agencies
- Therapists
- Friends
- Your mom

Tips for Ensuring a Successful Relationship:

- Prepare for your meetings ahead of time
- Listen to advice with an open mind; then make your own decision
- Respect one another's boundaries
- Remember that it is a relationship – and every relationship must be mutually beneficial
- Establish good communication habits
- Maintain the relationship proactively for the long term

Some companies offer employees formal mentoring programs. Law firms, for example, often assign senior attorneys to work with specific younger attorneys. These senior attorneys teach the younger ones how to do their research, introduce them to key people inside the firm, include them in networking opportunities with clients and prospects, and help them chart their path toward partnership.

A mentor does not have to come from inside your own company or industry, however. In many cases it is helpful to have an outsider bring a fresh, unbiased perspective. This can be especially useful if you are dealing with sensitive client issues or office politics.

On the other hand, you might find that sometimes it's best to have someone who understands the unique challenges of your profession. Consider Julie, for example, who is a dermatologist trying to decide whether to remain in solo practice, form a partnership, or join a large clinic. There are many factors to consider, including how her decision will impact her financial and professional future, and her personal life. Other doctors who have faced similar career crossroads will be the best source of relevant advice for Julie.

Regardless of where you find a mentor, having one can help you stay focused on your career goals. Mentors help you read and understand the maps in that hypothetical cross-country drive. They help you navigate rough stretches because they have been there before. A good mentor is someone that looks upon your problems as minor pitfalls, while helping you make the most of new opportunities – and perhaps take chances you might otherwise pass up.

"The most powerful women networkers understand that it's not about what you can get, but what you can give. Walk into a room and ask yourself 'How can I serve this group of people today?' When you talk with someone new ask yourself 'Who do I know that I can introduce them to?' Efforts like these will always help you in the end, as well."

**Neen James**
**Productivity & Performance Expert**
**Doylestown, PA**

# Finding a mentor

If you want a structured mentoring relationship, then you need to give some advance thought to what such an arrangement involves. You may also have some concerns about selecting the right person, especially if you do not already have a logical person in mind.

Start by identifying the issues you feel you need a mentor to help you tackle. Then, determine the characteristics that your ideal mentor will have:

1. Should they have a specific type of business or industry experience?

2. How old do you think this person should be?

3. What do you expect them to provide for you?

4. Is their physical location an issue?

5. How often will you plan to meet?

Women sometimes face gender-specific challenges in the workplace, so it may be beneficial for you to seek out female mentors. While men can certainly be valuable mentors to female professionals, there are some issues to which they may not relate, and therefore may be unable to provide relevant guidance. As you create your "ideal mentor" list, ask yourself if gender is a factor.

---

**Louise is a 30-year-old CPA in a large firm. She has worked for the firm for seven years, and has consistently received praise for her work. Yet more than once she has been overlooked when senior partners are assigning important clients, and she's not sure she's on track to make partner. One of her male colleagues joked that the partners were probably just afraid that she would "run off and have a baby." Louise and her husband are planning to start a family in the near future, and she is now confused and frustrated by how this will affect her position at this firm. In this case, it's probable that an experienced woman can provide Louise a reality check more than a man could, giving her the insight and advice to make the best choices for her career and family.**

---

Brainstorm a list of people who meet your requirements for a mentor. This can be difficult, so take your time and try to include both people you know and people you know of. You may also need to reach out to your network to ask other people to make recommendations.

Then, take the plunge and ask. Be sure to find out whether that person would be receptive to a mentoring role. If the other person understands mentoring and is willing to discuss the idea with you, call to arrange an initial meeting. This mentoring relationship can be as formal and structured as needed – or it may be just a couple of conversations to help you figure something out. Be honest about how you see the relationship developing and the time commitment involved. Their experiences and advice will not only make you feel good, it will also allow you to grow and learn.

## What is a peer group?

In a nutshell, a peer group is made up of people at similar places in their careers that act as a personal advisory board for one another. Peer groups can be an important part of your network, as they provide you with a trusted group of colleagues that you can turn to for advice, resources, introductions and support. Many entrepreneurs use this model to share best practices. Ideally, peer groups are an open and safe environment in which to test business ideas, discuss challenges and opportunities, and to gain honest feedback.

As with mentors, peer groups can be informal, occasional gatherings of select people, or a more formal organization with dues, bylaws, and specific membership requirements. In some cities, the local chamber of commerce organizes formal peer groups for business owners to meet other like-minded business owners. The Entrepreneurs Organization, The Alternative Board, and the Global Alliance for Women also do this for their members.

Fairly recent to the scene is an organization for entrepreneurial women that combines peer groups, networking events, and online networking. Ladies Who Launch connects women online and in person to foster creativity, community, and support. It is a business training program for women who want to launch their own business that focuses more on mutual support and inspiration than the technical side of business ownership. Ladies Who Launch offers members an online network, regular regional conferences, an online magazine, and a blog. Members can also participate in an "Incubator" that puts ten women (all of whom are either starting or expanding a business) into an intense four-week program, creating a very powerful peer group. Upon completion of the Incubator program, these women become a part of the Ladies Who Launch Network. Nancy Livingstone, a member of Ladies Who Launch in Los Angeles, describes the benefits of membership this way: "The Incubator was a kick in the pants, but it's the ongoing community that really keeps the fires burning."

## Organizing your own peer group

Finding the right people to be a part of a peer group is similar to finding a mentor. While some people may be obvious, it's important to include those who are not already your close friends. Start by identifying two or three people you already know who are committed to growing their network and advancing their career. Include people who are outside of your industry or profession, as you will learn most by having a diversity of skills and experiences in your group.

Then, build the group by having each member look at their own contact lists and adding one or two more. Limit this to between ten and fifteen people; peer groups function best in smaller numbers. This allows for some attrition while keeping it small enough for everyone to really get to know one another and actively participate in meetings. While it's not crucial to keep the group's existence a secret, it is preferable because it prevents others from asking to join. Once the group begins meeting, it's difficult to add people because of all the time that has been invested early on, and the trust and chemistry that already have been built amongst the participants.

Be sure to set the ground rules for your peer group early. Decide how often you should meet, and ask all members to make the commitment. If someone's work or travel schedule is irregular and does not allow them to make most meetings, find someone else. As with a mentor relationship, confidentiality is a must. Discuss this at your first meeting, and get buy-in on the rules and structure of your peer group.

Make sure that everyone gets a chance to talk about themselves during the first few meetings; peer groups are not a place for people to stay on the sidelines and observe. One option is for each member to have the focus of a meeting to discuss his or her issues. While you can meet with members of your peer group one-on-one, the group dynamic can be very beneficial when you are wrestling with a problem or analyzing the pros and cons of an opportunity. An idea or opinion from one member of your peer group might spawn an idea from another member, leading to a creative and productive session.

For the group to succeed, everyone must make attending and actively participating a priority. Keep in mind that even with a successful set of people who develop close relationships, the group will eventually play itself out. That's just fine; it has served its purpose and chances are, the friendships developed within the peer group will last.

## Thom Says:

I've had several good mentors. Some were formal mentoring relationships and some were informal, but having people understand my goals and aspirations and be willing to step up and provide advice has been invaluable. At one point in my career I felt that I needed an official mentor relationship with a seasoned community leader. I was still relatively young and unsure how to approach the right person. Glenn was the former head of the local chamber of commerce and someone who had built a solid reputation. I approached another community leader whom I knew well and discussed my motivation for wanting to get to know Glenn better. She reached out to him and had the initial discussion, encouraging him to be my mentor.

While we only met one-on-one a few times, I would often run into him at networking events and other functions. His counsel helped guide me through some tough times in my career, and the feeling that he always had my best interest at heart was reassuring.

If you want a mentor but do not have a specific person in mind, ask people you respect for suggestions. You will be surprised how quickly you can identify someone who could fill this role and guide you to higher levels of achievement.

## *Marny Says:*

After working with a public relations and marketing firm for eight years, I made the decision to hang my own shingle. To do so successfully, I felt I needed the support and camaraderie of other independent marketing professionals. A good friend left a similar role about the same time and we agreed that we needed a peer group. We each identified several independent marketing professionals, and those individuals then reached out to people within their networks. We ended up with eight members that included a graphic designer, an Internet marketer, a high-tech public relations professional, a market research professional, a copy writer, and an events planner.

Our all-female peer group met about once a month and discussed everything from fee structures and problem clients to office rental rates and sub-contractors, and eventually personal matters such as career-life balance and child care options. As trust was built among us, we began referring business and even pursuing potential clients together. The group has evolved over time; some members have moved on and new ones have joined, but the group as a whole remains a valuable resource and support system for me.

# FAQ:

**I only have three years of professional experience; how can I be a mentor?**

Consider mentoring someone who is just starting out in your field, or who is still in school. You could also mentor someone who may have more years of experience than you, but is new to your company or your community. Your experiences thus far qualify you to help others; don't sell yourself short.

**My mentor is not what I'd envisioned; how do I make this work?**

Make sure you have clearly defined and articulated the kind of assistance you would like from your mentor; there simply may be a communication problem. Try beginning your next meeting by reiterating your goals, and determining if you can meet them together. If not, it should be clear to both of you that the mentoring has not worked out in this particular pairing. That's okay. Move on.

**Where should our peer group meet?**

Choose somewhere private and quiet, so that you can have meaningful discussions and confidentiality. Peer group members can rotate hosting meetings in their homes, places of business, or in a private room in a restaurant. Choose a venue that is conveniently located for all participants.

**I like some people in my peer group more than others; how do I handle that?**

It is natural that you click with some members more than others. It is important, however, that you behave professionally with all of the people in your peer group, and that you are inclusive and supportive. Even if your relationships with a few members become more important and mutually beneficial, work hard to avoid cliques developing within your peer group.

**My mentor intimidates me; she is such a mover and shaker that I can't relate to her at all. How do I get her to take it down a notch for me?**

First, thank your lucky stars that someone so influential has agreed to be your mentor. Next, pat yourself on the back since you are clearly worthy of such a relationship. Try to take advantage of the counsel and connections she brings, even if it means stretching beyond your comfort zone. If the advice she gives and the opportunities she presents are beyond your current capabilities, encourage her to give you more attainable goals, being as specific as possible and very, very thankful for her efforts.

# 10

# NETWORKING WITH SOCIAL MEDIA

While people are still people, the tools we use to communicate have changed over the past several generations. Our great-grandparents were born into a world where local and face-to-face conversations were the main way of sharing information. While these type of relationships are still vitally important, today we are connected to people all over the world and we have instant access to information.

Since the arrival of the Internet in our daily lives, people communicate and connect with others around the world in what has become a vast web of ways to share information: one-to-one, small group or mass communications. Where the term "networking" could once only apply to building and cultivating connections with those whom you could meet in person or over the telephone, almost everyone on the planet is now within reach.

This changes everything, but it is important to remember that tech tools do not replace the power of in-person conversation.

## What is Social Networking?

There are many ways that people can find each other online, but the domination of the social media sites has received a lot of attention from individual subscribers, investors, and the media. Facebook, LinkedIn, Twitter, YouTube, SnapChat, Instagram and others offer people the chance to make, grow, and keep their business relationships. The ways in which we are connected to others has changed and it will never go back.

In 2006 Rupert Murdoch's News Corp. purchased MySpace for $580 million. The MySpace phenomenon had taken hold with teenagers and college students, but was also heavily used by business professionals and musicians to create virtual brochures about themselves in an effort to reach others who share similar interests. But their day in the sun was short-lived.

Facebook soon took over the spotlight in 2007, and has since become the main site for people to connect and cultivate relationships. While many people still wonder why anyone would want this much contact with their friends, our society is becoming more accustomed to this type of communications. As of the writing of this edition Facebook has over 1.4 billion users worldwide. If Facebook were a country, it would have the largest population in the world. When we released the original edition of this book there were 100 million subscribers. That is a huge increase in just seven years.

At first, social media was considered a personal tool for the younger generations, but now people of all ages participate in online networking. Social media is not a fad, and those who continue to avoid participation are going to feel more isolated.

Professionals who want to communicate with a broad audience and who are trying to position themselves as thought leaders should be using Twitter. Like all online social networking sites, it is not for everyone, but for some it has been a valuable tool for meeting new people and developing relationships.

Here are some common uses for networking sites:

- Friends who want to chat online
- Brands that want to keep in touch with customers
- Professionals seeking new employment
- Professional search firms sourcing new candidates for clients
- Business professionals doing research
- Celebrities who want to stay top of mind

- Politicians who want to communicate with constituents

- People who want to connect their friends with other friends for business or personal reasons

- Business people and co-workers interested in networking

- Classmates and study partners

Social media and digital networking tools have become commonplace in all areas of human engagement. There are more and more tools popping up online as apps for our phones and tablets, and the trend will not slow down. The need for human-to-human connection and a desire to belong to communities is part of our DNA, and as technologies continue to change even more tools will appear.

## LinkedIn

For business professionals there is simply no excuse not to have a profile on LinkedIn. LinkedIn has emerged as the premier business site and in the past several years has grown to nearly 400 million users (that is larger than the entire population of the United States). All professionals should have a profile on LinkedIn, regardless of industry, job type or experience level. It has become common for people to search the site in advance of a meeting to look for things they may have in common with those with whom they will be conversing. It is easier than using a Google search, since if a person has a common name that method might bring up too many choices. By using LinkedIn you are more likely to find the person you are looking for because the system will take into account your geography and mutual connections and prioritize the person you are searching for above others with the same name. You will also find more relevant information about their professional life, rather than photos of their kid's latest birthday party.

Many shy away from wanting to have their résumé information on LinkedIn, but as the site has become more popular, those who use it expect others to be present. When they search and cannot find you, they may determine that you are out of touch with the largest online business social networking tools.

Those who regularly read the profiles of people they are doing business with will often discover things in common, mutual friends, and background information that allow them to not only forge friendships faster, but also uncover ways to better serve the other person's needs. Not utilizing LinkedIn means you are missing out on delivering at your highest potential. Keep in mind that LinkedIn and other online social networking sites and apps are not just about promoting yourself; they are a research tool.

## Blogging

Blogging is another online networking and branding activity that became popular a decade ago, but remains a powerful way to reach your network by sharing your thoughts with the world. Bloggers will regularly publish posts that are relevant to their industry or other special interests. When a blog has regular readers, these fans will often comment on the topics and thus help create an open discussion on the site. Many bloggers develop a following and a community amongst their group of readers. Some blogs have just a few readers, with others having millions of people who follow the stories, advice, and pontifications of the blog owner. If done correctly, a blog is a great credibility tool to help you promote yourself or your business.

## Podcasting

Podcasting is also a great digital networking tool. A podcast is a radio-style show that can be accessed via iTunes, Stitcher, individual websites or other platforms and listened to at any time. Like a blog, it allows the host to reach many people in their network with information, ideas, interviews, etc., and to build a following and grow their reputation. Those who host interview-style shows have found that it can be an amazing tool to reach people you might not be able to contact. Many are flattered if you ask them to be a guest on your show. Thom, for example, started the "Cool Things Entrepreneurs Do" podcast in 2014 and had the chance to meet many people through this medium. Both guests on his show and other podcasters became part of his network, and over time led to being friends and referral sources for his business. While podcasting has been around for a long time, it became wildly popular in the last few years, and should continue to grow in relevance in 2016 and beyond when new cars will come with podcast delivery platforms as standard equipment with their sound systems.

# Twitter

When the first edition of *Some Assembly Required: A Networking Guide for Women* was released in 2008, Twitter was a relatively new micro-blogging site where people shared their thoughts in 140 characters or less. This popular site has now become part of the world-wide culture, with presidents, prime ministers, business leaders, celebrities, musicians, corporate brands, and even the Pope using Twitter as a way to communicate with followers. It has become one of the most popular ways for people to share ideas. While there are still skeptics who see Twitter as an ongoing waste of time, many professionals find it to be a valuable tool.

# Why is social media important to you?

As with anything popular, you need to know what tools
others are using. Even if you are not actively using online
social networking sites for your own contacts, you want
to have a basic understanding of their services and who is
using them. While there is no "best" social media platform,
you can get most of your professional needs met with
LinkedIn. If you have been resistant to opening an account,
the time has come. While this is not a magic bullet that
will bring you career success, you should not be invisible to
your business community; in fact, you may be conspicuous
by your absence. If you think you may want a new job or
that you could get laid off, LinkedIn is a must-have, since
recruiters and HR departments look to LinkedIn as a way
to vet candidates. If you wait until you are out of work to
set up your account you will be behind, as it takes time to
cultivate your contacts and fine-tune your profile.

Once you launch your account, or update your profile, you
will be surprised how many people you already know will
discover your profile and send you invitations to join their
networks.

Social networking sites are a great tool for finding former
business colleagues, and are a fast way to search for and
reconnect with those with whom you have lost touch. When
Thom was asked to be linked to a college fraternity brother
via LinkedIn, he discovered that the other person's network
included dozens of old friends. It was great to be able to

exchange emails with them and learn about their lives and careers three decades later. Many had jobs in industries that were complementary to his, and by reconnecting he could also tap into future business opportunities.

Over time you will discover that these online communities are a great way to rekindle and cultivate relationships. Reading the status updates of friends and sharing your own information creates a conduit for not losing touch. It used to be that once we moved on in our lives we would never re-encounter those old friends who did not live in our same geographic region, but now there is no excuse for not keeping connected.

The professional benefits of these online networking sites can be many if their membership includes the demographics of those with whom you wish to connect. However, like any community, you have to invest time to understand the protocol and proper etiquette of how to interact within the site. And each social networking site is a little different.

Social networking communities can also make it easier for you to regularly review your contacts and view their current career status. People change jobs often and it is easy to lose touch with people when their email address and phone numbers change. If they keep their online profile up to date then you will instantly have access to their new information. Some sites even offer functionality that alerts you when your contacts update their profiles.

These sites also make it simple for you to see whom your contacts are connected with. Sometimes these connections are kept private, but often they are viewable. By regularly reviewing the lists of whom your friends are connected to, you can identify business professionals whom you'd like to meet and can ask for an introduction. The process also works in reverse; if there is an individual you are looking to meet, you can trace the connection path back to your network. Often you will be surprised that the one person who can make the important introduction is someone you regularly speak with.

Just as importantly, if you keep your profile updated, your network can find you when you make a change. Your public profile on these popular websites makes it extremely easy for other people to locate you, and you don't want to miss valuable opportunities simply because they don't know where you work these days.

Recruiters also use these tools to find candidates for job openings. Always reply to recruiters, even if you are not interested in the job opportunity they are presenting. Recruiters can be amazing contacts for you, and for others in your network. Just because you are not interested in a career change today, that may not be the case in a few years. Be excited when you return the call or email and listen to what they have to say. If you are not interested, let them know, but always find out the complete details of the job they are trying to fill. You might know someone who would be an ideal fit, and both the recruiter and the other person would benefit from your making an introduction.

If you fail to have the common courtesy of returning their phone call, they may overlook you in the future. Additionally, it's a good practice to ask the recruiter questions about the focus of their business and let them know that you would be willing to help them make connections for any future searches that they are working on. If they live in your same town, invite them to join you for coffee or lunch.

Online networking is an incredibly valuable tool to expand your geographic reach. For example, try looking for people you want to know in a city you will be visiting by using social media to get advance introductions to key individuals in that city. Before arriving, schedule coffee, lunch, and dinners with new people so that you can build your network on a national or even international basis. By planning ahead, you can keep your calendar full while traveling and maximize your networking opportunities.

When Thom's daughter chose her college he wanted to uncover business opportunities in that new area so that he could go visit her more often. He utilized Facebook, LinkedIn, Twitter, and his podcast to reach out to interesting people in the area. He was quick to discover mutual friends and garner introductions to key business leaders in the area. While it will take time for him to cultivate business, he instantly had conversations, and was able to set up face-to-face meetings for each of his visits. Over time he is confident this will lead to his finding more clients that will bring him to town.

## Social Media Caveats

Online networking is not the same as face-to-face networking. Adding someone to your online community does not make them your "instant friend." Real friendships are developed over time and require the discovery of both mutual interests and shared experiences. Many people who do not enjoy the whole concept of networking will often look to social media as a replacement for building relationships the old-fashioned way. They look at their number of contacts and feel confident that they are doing a good job of creating a network. This may or may not be the case.

Just because you have a digital link does not mean that the other person will be invested in the relationship – in fact, to them, you may not even have a relationship. It is very difficult to know someone by just reading his or her profile. Working in the same industry or having similar interests is not enough for a strong, mutually beneficial business relationship.

Different people have different policies regarding the use of social networking sites. While some people will link to anyone and everyone, others believe that the sites are tools to expand our networks with people with whom we can have real connections. We fall into the latter group. We do not believe in open networks (connecting to everyone who breathes air). In the same way that having a copy of a the Los Angeles County phone book does not mean that you have 10 million people in your network, being linked to strangers does not make them part of your network. We suggest you do not link to anyone you have not spent time with over a cup of coffee or a beer, or at least with a lengthy phone call. We call this the "Coffee, Call or Beer Rule," and it ensures that people will actually remember you should the need come to contact them at a later date. Before adding people to your social media lists, make sure there is a reason and a foundation for a possible relationship.

Maintaining a large online social network can take a huge amount of time. Some people are "link collectors" and will never contact you. Others will inundate you with email and other spam. To some folks, having a digital link means that they will send you email on any number of subjects. Since you do not know them personally, their messages will most likely just become more clutter in your inbox.

When we speak to business audiences on the topic of networking we will often get invitations to join the network of those in the audience. It is our belief that having lots of links to those that you do not really know dilutes the power of your network. Too many strangers in your network will clutter your contact lists and make it more time-consuming to find those you are looking for when you have a need. Keeping your contact lists lean will make you more efficient.

Since members in these online communities are not pre-screened or educated on the purpose of the service, you have no way of knowing the goals of people whom you might encounter. Just because someone has a profile on one of these sites does not mean they welcome everyone on the planet to contact them. Just as when you meet someone at a face-to-face event, you need to properly follow the steps to begin a conversation. Do not assume you have the right to call on them because you stumbled upon them online.

1. A relevant strategy, consistency and caution are keys to social media success.

2. Embrace online social networking as an important tool to help build your network.

3. Keep your profiles and contact information up to date so others can find you.

4. Value quality over quantity.

5. Only link to those whom you actually know.

6. Recognize the limits of trying to build relationships solely with social media.

7. Assume everything you post, like, pin or update will be read by everyone!

"I network both online and in person. I actively keep up with my LinkedIn contacts and regularly share information that I think would interest them. I send ecards on their birthdays, and regularly provide virtual introductions to connections I think can mutually help one another."

**Lisa Ong**

**Certified Executive Coach**

**Dallas, TX**

## Thom Says:

You have to have your own guidelines for utilizing social media and online networking tools. My rule is that I do not connect on LinkedIn or Facebook to people I have not had a real conversation with. But some people who send connection requests get upset that I won't accept their connection without a phone call. There is no reason to get upset; be respectful that different people use these tools differently.

## Marny Says:

As with traditional networking, there is no right or wrong reason to network via social media. To me, the important thing is that you actually think about why you are using social media, and what you are hoping to get out of it. For me, I use it to stay in touch with my network and to be able to find people that I used to know. It is just as important that they be able to easily find me if, for example, they have seen me speak at a conference but can't find my information, I want them to be able to plug in my name and be directed to my LinkedIn profile. It's also important to me that my social media profile is an effective and consistent branding tool. These are the factors that drive my personal choices on where and how to participate on social media.

# FAQ:

**When is the right time to connect with a new contact via LinkedIn?**

Sending someone you just met a LinkedIn request is a great next step in getting to know one another and beginning a professional relationship. Take a moment to look over their profile, and learn a little about their job and their background. Then send a request, adding a personal note that reminds them when/where you met. This is an especially good strategy when there wasn't an obvious next step in building a new relationship, as is often the case.

**What tips do you have for including photos in a profile?**

First, be sure to do it! Having a photo in today's increasingly visual society is important. It should be recent, clear and should focus on your face – no full body shots! It should also be professional in nature, which means no husbands, significant others, kids or pets in the photo please. A plain background, simple clothing and a warm smile will complete the picture and create the image you want.

**Is there really such a thing as having too many contacts on social media?**

Yes! Take a simple challenge. Go through the first 50 friends in your Facebook site or your first 50 connections in LinkedIn... if you find more than one or two people that you simply don't recognize by name or photo, you have too many connections! Remember the definition of networking – this definition applies online as well as in person. If you couldn't reach out and ask these people for help (or offer it) then they are not a true connection.

**Is it appropriate and effective to have business contacts on Facebook?**

Yes! If you have come to know and like someone, there is no reason to exclude them from your Facebook account. Sometimes people worry about business contacts seeing what they post online, but a good rule of thumb is never post anything you do not want your professional contacts to know about. People do business with those they know, like and trust. When you build real friendships in with those you know professionally you will find more success.

**How do you connect with former coworkers or friends whom you've lost touch with via social media?**

Reach out and say hello. Do not wait until you need them for a business purpose to make the connection. Use LinkedIn or Facebook and send them a note telling them you want to re-connect. If you had a good relationship in the past they will be happy to hear from you.

**11**

# NETWORKING FOR MOMS

It's an undeniable fact that becoming a mother changes everything in your life. It changes the way you look at the world, alters your priorities, and redefines your relationships with family and friends. Having children changes how you work and think about your career. We are fortunate to live today in a society where many women have choices when it comes to career and motherhood. While some women must work to support their families, others can choose whether or how to continue their career. Regardless of whether you decide to be a stay-at-home or full-time working mom (or something in between), networking must remain an active part of your life. Every woman benefits from building and maintaining connections, both professionally and personally.

**"For me, it was important to stay engaged in activities outside of my 'mother role' in order to explore possible new careers when the time came to go back to work. Many businesses don't advertise positions that are flexible and/or part-time, so remaining connected to a variety of people is key."**

**Emily Kosakowski**
**Clyfford Still Museum**
**Denver, Colorado**

# Keeping your network alive

What do networking and motherhood have to do with each other? Let's go back to our definition of networking from Chapter 1: Networking is the process of building and leveraging mutually beneficial relationships. Those relationships most definitely include both professional associates and personal friends. In fact, friendships with other mothers will be among the most important relationships in your life.

Some women find motherhood to be an isolating experience, especially if most of their friendships were developed in the workplace. Women today start their families at all different ages, and you may be in a different stage of your life than your closest friends. This can be hard, as you now may have less in common with the women who were formerly your confidants. But it is also a great time to develop new friendships with women who have children the same age as your own.

Other mothers can be a source of endless information, ideas, advice and support. With the mommy network, you can exchange information not only related directly to child development (Has Joshua started teething yet? At what age did Jenna drop her morning nap? How did Riley handle the transition into middle school?), but also on the child-related services and products on which we all rely. You can ask your network about babysitters, pediatricians, baby gates, gymnastics classes, pre-schools, family-friendly vacations, etc. Yet even more important than these tips is the support and advice you will get from and give to women who are sharing the ups and downs of motherhood. Just having other moms to talk to can make a big difference.

Regardless of whether you're continuing to work or staying at home for an indeterminate amount of time, it's crucial to maintain your network of professional contacts. If you have made the choice to take a hiatus from the workforce, remember that you never know when you'll be working again. You might want (or need) to go back to work sooner than you think, or you might want to change to a more family-friendly profession or company, or start your own business. You'll need the relationships that you cultivated earlier in your career to help you find a new job, new clients, employees, partners, or other opportunities. Unfortunate as it may be, it is also a hard reality that many mothers find themselves re-entering the workforce because of a change in their family's financial situation or a divorce. It's an arduous process to build an entirely new network, so don't let yours deteriorate just because you have stepped out of wage-earning mode. Your network is a valuable asset and you must make it a priority to keep it alive.

**Dana, a former professional fundraiser for the performing arts, had spent the last seven years as a stay-at-home-mom. Unfortunately, she and her husband divorced. She had a terrific network of friends, neighbors, and other parents, and had been an active volunteer in her community and in her children's school. But she had let her professional relationships in the fundraising community fade away. Dana had to work hard at rebuilding her network; she reconnected with old employers and colleagues, and reached out to her personal contacts for ideas and introductions. It was a difficult transition, but by working hard to create new professional relationships, she did eventually find a good position. It would have been easier had she never let her professional network lapse.**

Networking is also challenging for women trying to balance work and family, especially if they're handling the demands of both for the first time. Networking can be time consuming, and it can be tempting to reduce or eliminate it to spend more time with your children. Women who view networking as a non-essential activity will probably do just that. But those who understand the long-lasting impact that networking can have on their career also know that there are ways to include strategic networking in your schedule. Lunch, anyone?

The key is to identify and prioritize the people, organizations, and events that are the most critical to your career. You cannot do it all, but you must do some things to maintain your visibility in your business community; remain committed to the most relevant and critical organizations and events. If you plan and prioritize your networking strategy, you'll be fine.

## A new kind of networking

While becoming a mother may pose some limits to your networking, it also offers new opportunities. Power lunches at hot new restaurants and cocktail parties at trendy bars appear in your calendar with less regularity. But play dates and birthday parties can lead to much more than you might think, on both the professional and personal fronts.

Neighborhood groups, schools, and religious organizations all offer ways to connect with others, as do organized activities such as baseball or ballet. It can be even easier to initiate and grow relationships in this way than in a business setting, as you instantly have something in common – your kids.

Consider the following neighborhood, community, and parent organizations that may offer great mommy networking:

- Play groups – provide moms the chance to gather together and let their kids play while they engage in adult conversation

- Dinner clubs – enable parents to have adult time with regular gatherings of friends or neighbors

- Bunko/Book clubs – give moms a fun activity to do with other moms, generally monthly

- PTA – provide volunteer opportunities in your children's school, a great way to have the double win of being involved with your children's education and working on projects with other moms

- Religious groups – offer church-, synagogue- and other religious-based programs for parents, including social and educational

Leadership opportunities also abound in community and school organizations, so your skills and experience don't have to slide. Pursue volunteer positions with committees and boards of directors; many arrange meetings around parents' schedules. You may have to seek out participation in these groups, as they are generally less formally organized than business organizations. Know, however, that many groups of this type do not operate as efficiently as professional associations or for-profit companies. You may be able to make a significant contribution as an experienced volunteer or businesswoman. Don't be discouraged if it takes a little time to figure out how to get involved. As with any organization, it may also take a while to really connect with others in these groups, but with persistent contributions, you will make it work. All of the networking techniques discussed in the previous chapters work as well with a Girl Scout troop as with a professional association, so put them to work for you.

---

Leslie, this book's editor, became pregnant with her first child in 1997. During her second trimester, she joined a listserv for women expecting a baby in February 1998. Over the last 11 years the Feb Moms have shared birth stories, personal and professional milestones, plus enough parenting Q&A to fill several gigabytes of Wikipedia. They have supported each other as marriages crumbled, as cancer diagnoses were handed out, and as families moved across the country and around the globe. At its peak, its membership reached into the hundreds; for the last five years it has remained a stable group of 20 women living on three continents.

From time to time, subsets of the Feb Moms get together in person when one travels to another person's area for business or pleasure. And for Leslie's 40th birthday, five of them spent a long weekend in Savannah, exploring a city none had ever been to. Tory, a university librarian in Hong Kong, gave an insider's tour to Leslie and her family when they visited Eastern Asia several years back.

**After Leslie had been an active participant for four years, she and another member, Jen, realized that they worked in the same industry, lived within 20 miles of each other, and even had mutual friends. In fact, Jen's husband participates in an annual philanthropic bike race, and as the pack of bikers pass Leslie's house, Leslie and her children are there in their pajamas, cheering Charles on.**

**This is mommy networking at its best.**

## The Mommy Wars

When it comes to being a working mother, today's women have many more choices than did the women of previous generations. Long gone are the days when women's job choices were limited to wife, mother, and housekeeper, and perhaps teacher or nurse. Gone also is the Super Woman mentality of the 1980s, when women were expected to pursue high-powered careers in lieu of staying home with children. Even the cultural shift in the 1990s toward being a full-time "soccer mom" seems to have abated, with women instead pursuing a wide variety of options for the personal and professional roles they play.

Today's range of options, however, seems to be a double-edged sword. With mothers choosing so many different paths, it is increasingly common to find women judging the decisions of other mothers quite harshly. The Mommy Wars pit full-time working moms against full-time stay-at-home moms, both privately and publicly. Each side is vehement in its beliefs, creating a right-or-wrong scenario that actually serves no one.

In March of 2015, Fortune.com ran a story that captured media attention and spawned debate across the country. In this story Katharine Zaleski, cofounder & president of PowerToFly, the first global platform matching highly skilled women with tech positions they can do from home, apologized to all the mothers she had worked with. In an honest letter, Zaleski admitted that she silently questioned working mothers' work ethics, doubted their commitment, and scheduled last-minute 4:30 meetings without ever considering that parents might need to pick up their kids at daycare. She didn't support working moms with male colleagues. She states that she didn't realize how horrible she had been – until she had a child of her own. She now realized that professional women were still somewhat trapped between being a full-time professional or a full-time mom. And she wanted to give them a third choice. Today, Zaleski realizes that value and productivity is not in the number of hours logged in an office, but in work completed. And she apologized to working moms – working parents, for that matter – for not recognizing that earlier in her career. She points out that over 80% of women will become mothers by age 44 (according to the US Census Bureau) and challenges work cultures to understand this and adapt. This story clearly shows the challenges that still exist for working mothers, but more and more options and opportunities are being created.

## Combining both worlds

One gray area in the Mommy Wars is the women who do not fall into either the stay-at-home or the working mother camp. Instead, they have found ways to continue their professional life while being a hands-on parent, too. Consider the following examples of mothers who are a new kind of tweener:

- Natalie left her position at a large accounting firm to join a small, local firm with more flexible hours.

- Celia is job-sharing a full-time position as a physical therapist with another mom, each working half-time.

- Beth chose to leave her management position with a department store until her daughter starts kindergarten, but continues to consult on an hourly basis with her former employer on specific projects.

- Layla left her full-time position with an ad agency and began working from home as a freelance graphic designer, placing her son in a nearby day care three days a week.

Not every mother has the luxury of working part-time, working from home, working for herself, or job-sharing.

But more and more women are realizing the power they hold in the workforce and are expecting that their career and employers will provide them with the flexibility to balance work and parenting more effectively. Many women have ten years or more of valuable experience in their careers before starting a family, and this is leading to more options. In 2007, the Bureau of Labor Statistics reported that nearly 26% of working women with children under age 18 work flexible schedules, as compared with 14% in 1991. In addition, the number of companies allowing employees to work remotely occasionally (telecommuting) saw an increase to 67% in 2014 from 50% in 2008, according to a survey by the Families and Work Institute.

Juggling a part-time job and the responsibilities of the primary caregiver may leave you feeling that you have no time for networking. This can be short sighted, and those who have found ways to work limited professional schedules still need to make networking a priority. You can find ways to stay current with your contacts and continue to meet new people.

## Women's Online Organizations

1) www.w2wlink.com

2) www.groups.yahoo.com/group/
   LinkedinPowerWomen

3) www.iVillage.com

4) www.ewomennetwork.com

5) www.ladieswholaunch.com

6) www.bellaonline.com

7) www.womenworking.com

8) www.womenbloom.com

## Thom Says:

When my older daughter was born, the plan was for my wife to quit her job and become a full-time mom. However, while Sara was on maternity leave, her manager offered her the promotion she had been working toward for five years. This left us with a bunch of choices on how we would balance career and family. In the end, we decided it'd be best for me to become my daughter's primary caregiver. This was an agonizing decision for us at the time, but one that led to many amazing experiences.

Before making the leap, I sought counsel from my mentors and other people in my network. Although no one I queried about this had actually done it, most people encouraged me.

At the same time, several people cautioned that it could kill my career, and that future employers might never respect my choice. In fact, the opposite has proven to be true, and the experience has given me a much better perspective on life and career.

During the time that I was out of the full-time, paid workforce, I continued to network. I regularly had coffee or lunch with former co-workers and clients. I did encounter people who looked down on my decision to stay home with Jackie, but I never let those people get to me. In fact, I continued to keep a high profile around the business community and attended business events with Jackie in tow. Sure, I was subject to the disapproving glances of some, but I was also careful to only bring Jackie along when it would not be disruptive.

My two years out of the workforce did not cause me any career setbacks, but instead was just one chapter in my life. I made sure that my network was strong and well-maintained, and when I was ready to return to work, people hadn't forgotten about me, nor me them.

## *Marny Says:*

As someone who works part-time and is a full-time mom, I am a tweener. And I sometimes find it isolating. Don't get me wrong; I am remarkably lucky to have the type of career, family and financial situation that provides me the option to work part-time. I love my work and I love working for myself out of a home office. But it can be also be somewhat tough to connect to some of the other moms, as I often don't feel like I fit into either the stay-at-home or the working mom camp.

Tweeners are a growing segment of mothers, and it's a lifestyle that is gaining momentum. My prediction is that there will soon be enough part-time working moms to create their own camp... but this is the last thing I want. I certainly benefit by knowing all kinds of mothers and learning from their different viewpoints and experiences. I believe that there shouldn't really be any camps at all. We all belong to the coolest club on the planet  motherhood  and that should connect us, regardless of our career choices and life necessities.

# FAQ:

**I work full time now but I'd like to work part time. How do I find legitimate part-time opportunities?**

This is a challenge for many moms that want to spend more time with their family. Your first step should be to reach out to your network (obviously!). Let them know the type of positions you are interested in and how you are qualified. Also, there are more and more websites that are tailor made for moms looking for part-time or flex-time positions, so get online!

**Many of my friends are now at home with kids while I still work full time. How do we bridge the gap and remain friends?**

Friendships are always evolving, and major differences in lifestyle like this can be difficult. Focus on the things you have in common, and find ways to spend time together. This will require compromises on both sides and perhaps a shift in expectations. You might have to work around nap time, or meet at kid-friendly restaurants, while they will have to understand you can't stop by in the afternoon for iced tea, or make every birthday party. Little things, like phone calls and e-mails, can help you stay connected even when face-to-face time is more limited.

**Is it possible to work from home and also tend to my baby?**

It is possible, but not easy! It depends on the type of work you do, and even the type of baby. If you need to talk on the phone, a fussy baby will make that nearly impossible, but if you do a majority of your work online, it will be easier. The most challenging part will be finding the time to focus on work with kids in the house. You can consider having a sitter in your home a few days a week (or a few hours a day) to help with this.

**I find volunteering at my child's school boring and the mothers there uninteresting. How do I find like-minded mothers to hang out with?**

Identify the activities or causes that you are interested in and get involved with groups that focus on those – you are bound to meet other moms that way. You can also join groups that are springing up all over the country designed to help moms network with one another. And try coordinating a gathering of your current mom friends, asking them to each bring another mom friend – this is a quick way to multiply your network!

**I am expecting my first baby; how do I find the time to be a mom, work, and continue my involvement with organizations?**

The key will be to prioritize your time and commitments... and chances are your baby will be your number one priority! As you make this transition in your life, you shouldn't try to do it all, but you are wise to keep networking as a priority. Determine which organization is the most important to your career and your network, and maintain your involvement there. Be prepared to temporarily scale back on other activities, and find other, less time-consuming ways to stay in touch.

# Conclusion

Networking is an important component of professional success regardless of gender. It can also play a major role in helping you achieve personal fulfillment. Critical relationships and exciting opportunities are developed every day as a direct result of networking. Because people do business with those that they know and like, rapport and trust are important for everyone to focus on while developing a positive reputation and real, lasting relationships. We hope that this book has helped you understand some of the mysteries of how to make, grow, and keep your business relationships.

Women need not run from or protest the differences that appear in the business world, but instead embrace their unique strengths and jump right into cultivating friendships that can, and will, lead to more business successes. As today's women deal with issues including work/family balance, the glass ceiling, the good ol' boy network, and the mommy wars, support networks are more important than ever.

People with large, functional networks understand that other people are a valuable resource. Like saving money in the bank for a rainy day while simultaneously earning interest, your network is an investment in your future. Seasoned networkers enjoy finding ways to help others without regard to any immediate pay-off. Networking should be fun and rewarding in the short term as well as over the long haul.

In order for networking to be effective, it must become a part of your lifestyle. Tangible results may not happen overnight, and it's undeniable that women have many responsibilities that compete for the limited hours of each day. Yet investing in the cultivation of powerful relationships will lead to connections, friendships, and future opportunities that you may never have dreamed of. So set your goals, make your plan, assemble your tools, and get out there and network!

# The Authors

**Marny Lifshen** is an author, speaker and marketing communications consultant with more than 25 years of experience. She works with businesses and executives to develop brand awareness and credibility with key audiences, and to establish relationships with key influencers.

In 2009, Marny was named a winner of the Profiles in Power and Women of Influence Awards hosted by the Austin Business Journal. She is a nationally recognized expert on strategic networking, communication and personal branding.

She is a seasoned keynote speaker and workshop leader for corporate, association and university clients across the country. Marny customizes the content and format of each program to address the specific goals of the client.

Marny's areas of expertise include:

- Strategic Networking

- Personal Branding

- Building Productive and Positive Professional Relationships

- Improving Professional Relationships Between the Genders

- Communicating Effectively with Colleagues

Marny regularly contributes to a variety of online and print publications. She is a proud graduate of the University of Texas. She lives in Austin, Texas with her husband, Mike, and their two daughters.

Marny can be reached at marnyl@austin.rr.com. Her website is www.marnylifshencommunications.com.

**Thom Singer** has an eclectic background working in sales, marketing and business development roles for Fortune 500 Companies, Law Firms, and entrepreneurial ventures. He believes that all opportunities come from people, and when we work together to find "cooperative significance" with others we all discover more success.

Singer is a professional master of ceremonies, speaker, trainer, consultant and the author of eleven books on the power of business relationships, business development, entrepreneurship, legal marketing and presentation skills. He speaks regularly at business and association conferences around the United States and beyond.

He is also the host of the widely popular "Cool Things Entrepreneurs Do" podcast. On this show he interviews entrepreneurs, solopreneurs, and business leaders from a variety of industries. He encourages his guests to share tips and ideas that can help those with an "entrepreneurial spirit" find their own path toward success.

Thom and his wife, Sara, make their home in Austin, Texas and are the parents of two highly spirited daughters.

CPSIA information can be obtained
at www.ICGtesting.com
Printed in the USA
FSOW04n1141260916
25419FS